Nineteenth-Century

AMERICAN MUSICAL
THEATER

General Editor
DEANE L. ROOT
University of Pittsburgh

A GARLAND SERIES

===== VOLUME 12 =====

Early Operetta in America

The Doctor of Alcantara *(1879)*

MUSIC BY JULIUS EICHBERG, LIBRETTO BY BENJAMIN E. WOOLF

Edited by
Charlotte R. Kaufman
New England Conservatory of Music

GARLAND PUBLISHING, INC.
NEW YORK AND LONDON 1994

Library of Congress Cataloging-in-Publication Data
Eichberg, Julius, 1824–1893.
  [Doctor of Alcantara. Vocal score]
  Early operetta in America : The doctor of Alcantara (1879)/ music by Julius
Eichberg, libretto by Benjamin E. Woolf; edited by Charlotte R. Kaufman.
  1 vocal score. cm.—(Nineteenth-century American musical theater; v. 12)
  Based on: Bon soir, Monsieur Pantalon / M. and Mme. Joseph Philippe Simon
Lockroy.
Reprint. Originally published. New, enlarg. and rev. ed. Boston : Oliver Ditson, c.
1879; libretto included in 1879 ed.
  ISBN 0-8153-1375-6
  1. Operas—Vocal scores with piano. 2. Operas—Librettos. I. Woolf, Benjamin
E. II. Lockroy, M., 1803-1891. Bon soir, Monsieur Pantalon. III. Eichberg,
Julius, 1824-1893. Doctor of Alcantara. Libretto. 1994. IV. Title. V. Series.
M1503.E4D6   1994   94–26277
                                                                          CIP

Book design by Patti Hefner

Contents

INTRODUCTION TO THE SERIES

This series of sixteen volumes provides for the first time ever a comprehensive set of works from a full century of musical theater in the United States of America. Many of the volumes contain musical scores and librettos that have never before been published. Others make available works that were long lost, or widely scattered, or never before assembled in one place. Collectively, this series is the first substantial modern printing, not only of the individual titles it contains, but also of a repertory that is central to the nation's cultural history.

The prevailing view of nineteenth-century American theater is dominated by attention to the *words* voiced by the actors. But for most of this period theater simply did not operate from written texts alone; music was an equal and essential partner with the script. Music was so ubiquitous in the American theater throughout the nineteenth century that any understanding of the subject—or of individual works or theaters, indeed even of specific performances or performers—must take it into account. Yet few scholarly studies and still fewer modern editions of works have included the music as fully as the text. (An excellent summary of recent research, and of the problems created by lack of access to original complete works, is presented in Shapiro, 1987.)

Moreover, this series should help balance an emphasis in the scholarly literature on the bibliography of pre-1800 works at one end and the history and criticism of twentieth-century shows at the other, by providing a substantial body of material in between. Almost without exception, the works published here have been unavailable—even unknown except by reputation—to all but a handful of specialists. As Joseph Kerman has pointed out in his book challenging the field of musicology, research on musical theater is forty years behind most of the western music genres in that its "central texts" (the works themselves) have remained unavailable (Kerman, 1985, p. 48). In a sense, this series is a throwback to an earlier style of anthology delineated by geographical, chrono-logical, and genre bounds, such as helped define historical national repertories for European scholars in the mid-twentieth century.

Until now, only a very few individual nineteenth-century musical-theater works have been issued in modern publications, sometimes—but not always—with the score alongside the libretto. Among the major scholarly series of editions that include musical-theater works performed in nineteenth-century America is A-R Editions' Recent Researches in American Music, which has made available William Shields's *The Poor Soldier* (1783), George F. Root's "operatic cantata" *The Haymakers* (1857), and Victor Pelissier's *Columbian Melodies* (1812) used in New York and Philadelphia theaters. A series from G.K. Hall, titled Three Centuries of American Music, has a single volume devoted to eighteenth- and nineteenth-century *American Opera and Music for the Stage* (1990), containing piano-vocal scores of Alexander Reinagle's *The Volunteers*, Rayner Taylor's *The Ethiop*, Arthur Clifton's *The Enterprise*, and Reginald de Koven's *Robin Hood*. And an English series of Music for London Entertainment 1660–1800, issued by Richard MacNutt (Tunbridge Wells) and later by Stainer & Bell (London), reproduces some works that were also performed in America.

Presented here by Garland Publishing, Inc., with full text and music, the forty-nine works in this series of sixteen volumes are now accessible not only to scholars of music, theater, literature, American studies, and other fields in the humanities and performing arts, but also to teachers and students in the classroom. Every work could be produced again on the stage, either as historic re-creation or in modern adaptation. The purpose of the undertaking is to make full works readily available for analysis, drama criticism, performance, and any other use by a modern academic audience as well as the general public.

The vast majority of surviving sources have lain scattered and hidden in public and private collections throughout the country, awaiting research that would piece them back together. At the time they were part of the living tradition of nineteenth-century American theater, such performance materials were considered functional and ephemeral. Their creators and users had little interest in preserving the works for posterity; they were much more mindful of the production at hand, of the business of attracting an audience and gaining its favor. If that meant keeping all the music scores in a trunk in a theater building prone to fire, or using scripts filled with up-to-the-minute changes, handwritten instructions, and typographical errors, or creating instrumental arrangements and musical insertions to the show without benefit of fully written-out scores, such were the necessities of life. Consequently they kept little, and published even less. (Sometimes their heirs, for whatever family interests they may have had, restricted access to the surviving sources for as much as a century. And even those materials that found their way into accessible archives have not been immune to loss by deterioration, misshelving, and pilferage.)

Most of the music that survives is in piano-vocal reduction from the theater-orchestra arrangements actually used. Much of it was printed and sold as souvenir selections for the musically literate public to use at leisure in their homes. Printed librettos were sold so that the audience could follow the performance at the theater.

This series strikes a balance between the more readily available printed piano-vocal selections and librettos, and the manuscript sources. In some cases, printed or manuscript musical excerpts have been reassembled to re-create a score the public never saw but which comes as close as possible to the melodies and harmonies that the theater musicians performed. In other volumes, the editors have drawn on contemporary sources to re-create the now-lost orchestration of the original theater arrangers (who would normally have been the resident conductors), or to assemble a full score from surviving orchestral parts. In only a few cases, original scores or librettos too indistinct or deteriorated to reproduce have been reset for clarity; we have sought to emphasize the value of seeing (reproducing) the *original* performance materials used in American theaters of the time. In every volume, the conditions of all known original sources and the circumstances surrounding their presentation in this series are clearly identified. Moreover, whenever possible the original sources are reproduced at actual size (although some have been altered slightly to fit the margins of modern printed books). Dates given in volume subtitles indicate the productions of the shows that generated the sources chosen to be reproduced.

The series aims to represent all the major genres and styles of musical theater of the century, from ballad opera through melodrama, plays with incidental music, parlor entertainments, pastiche, temperance shows, ethnic theater, minstrelsy, and operetta, to grand opera. These works reflect vividly the cultural mix of America: the incendiary *Uncle Tom's Cabin* stands alongside later shows written and performed by African-American troupes; the Irish and Yiddish theater in New York used language that modern audiences might not understand, but which was part of everyday life in the ghetto. At one end of the chronological spectrum we have shows imported by British immigrant musicians; at the other stands a grand opera written by the conductor of the Metropolitan Opera House, based on a great American novel.

The series General Editor has eschewed those titles, no matter how important, that are already available in full modern editions. Missing too are works, no matter how fine, of mostly local interest or regional significance. Nor is the series intended to suggest a core repertory, or a pantheon of masterworks. Rather, it is a selection of works by nineteen scholars active in research on a wide range of theatrical styles and cultural issues of the period.

Each volume of the series is complete in itself. Individual editors have each provided an introduction summarizing the careers and works of the composers and librettists. The introduction informs about the work(s) reproduced, giving dates and circumstances of first performances and any early revivals, origins of the plot and its treatment, and a brief critique explaining the historical importance of the work. The editors identify the locations of all significant original sources for each work, and any significant differences among them; they also note any other available performing materials that might be useful for a revival or detailed study (for example, a conducting score, other piano-vocal scores, instrumental parts, librettos, prompt books, stage designs, photographs, manuscript drafts). If the volume reproduces only a piano-reduction score, the editor's introduction identifies (as much as possible) the original instrumentation used in the theater. Recordings of any modern performances are mentioned, and a bibliography provides leads for further inquiry about the works and their creators. When necessary, notations have been made matching the musical selections of the score with their respective locations in the libretto.

Each volume editor has had principal responsibility for identifying the first or most appropriate copy available of the musical score and libretto. In selecting the copies to be reproduced, further preference has gone to those sources that are clean, untorn, and complete, which could be reprinted unedited. As is the nature of rare sources, the best exemplars are not always perfect ones, and we beg your patience with those that are less than ideal.

It is still true, as Anne Dhu Shapiro pointed out in 1987 (p. 570), that "the incomplete state of basic research in the area of musical theater . . . stands as the chief impediment to a better history." This series is offered with the hope and trust that it will foster greater understanding and contribute materially to the wider appreciation of America's heritage and traditions of musical theater.

Deane L. Root
University of Pittsburgh

WORKS CITED

Shapiro, Anne Dhu. Review of Julian Mates, *America's Musical Stage: Two Hundred Years of Musical Theatre*, in the *Journal of the American Musicological Society* XL/3 (Fall 1987): 565–74.

Kerman, Joseph. *Contemplating Music: Challenges to Musicology.* Cambridge, Mass.: Harvard University Press, 1985.

ABOUT THIS VOLUME

The Doctor of Alcantara is an intriguing work. It is the first score written on American soil by a composer who had participated in performances of the Offenbachian style of operetta in Europe. It enjoyed modest success before audiences for more than four decades, but then lapsed into obscurity and was almost completely unknown except to scholars for nearly a century.

What then was the significance of *The Doctor* to contemporary audiences? Was it the harbinger of a new era of musical theater, and on that merit deserving of an audience? Or was it more opportunistic, a pleasant but forgettable work that rode the coattails of theatrical fashion? The editor of this volume, Charlotte R. Kaufman, gives evidence that its greatest achievement was to counter the century-old injunction against staged musical theater in Boston.

The comic opera succeeded because it was tuneful, pleasant, and humorous. Written for actors who could sing, it relied on stage business and plot situations for its main interest. Most importantly, it was in English and it was chaste (though it poked fun at lovers' conceits and entanglements), which made it both intelligible and acceptable to middle-class audiences without fear of censure or condescension.

The book seems more contrived and the music no less distinctive than those of later works that owe something to the genre (see for example Sousa's *El Capitan* in Volume 14, and the burlesque *Evangeline* in Volume 13). Ms. Kaufman points out that the librettist, Benjamin Edward Woolf, has nonetheless been venerated beyond the composer, Julius Eichberg. Her introduction makes the case for a reappraisal of Eichberg's contributions.

Charlotte Kaufman is founder and director of The Friends of Dr. Burney, a vocal and instrumental ensemble that specializes in the performance of earlier musical theater and chamber opera, based on original source materials. She has prepared performing editions of several eighteenth-century ballad operas, and a critical edition of Jean-Jacques Rousseau's *Devin du Village* along with a companion volume of Dr. Charles Burney's English version, *The Cunning Man*. With The Friends of Dr. Burney, she has performed *The Doctor of Alcantara* at the Museum of Fine Arts, Boston, and elsewhere.

D. L. R.

This will be the first attempt made in this country to initiate a charming and popular character of light operatic entertainment, which at "Les Bouffes Parisiennes" in Paris, nightly attract the *ELITE* of the artistic world, and divides popularity with the leading places of amusement in that great city. (Handbill in Eichberg Scrapbooks, vol. 1, Boston Public Library)

Julius Eichberg's new operetta, *The Doctor of Alcantara*, opened at the Boston Museum on April 7, 1862. As the publicity announcement implies, this was a venture of some daring. Against heavy odds, Eichberg was pioneering a form of musical-theater entertainment in a city with an anti-theater atmosphere. However successful it might prove to be as art, *The Doctor of Alcantara* was significant as a social statement in the city of Boston.

In 1862 there still existed in Boston a uniquely hostile cultural climate with its roots in the previous century. The Puritans' Act of 1750 prohibiting theatrical performances had a lasting, deleterious effect on the city's theatrical and musical development, delaying even the stage debut of opera there. Boston lagged far behind Charleston, Providence, New York, and Philadelphia, which had all had operatic performances by the mid-eighteenth century. Boston's first professional operatic season began September 29, 1769, with the reading of *The Beggar's Opera* by a single performer who played all the parts and sang all the songs: the only way a theatrical performance could take place in Boston was in the form of a "reading" or "moral lecture" (McKay, pp. 133–134). Although the first official theater in Boston, a makeshift affair called The Board Alley, opened in 1792, the prohibitive act remained on the books until 1799.

Yet, Boston was a musically sophisticated city with no shortage of good singers and instrumentalists. According to music historian David McKay, although "Boston singers were consistently performing Handel's *Messiah*, musically no less demanding than the most difficult Italian opera—not a single opera was produced in Boston during the 1770s or 1780s. No attempt was made to encourage native composers. . ." (p. 140). Even after the re-opening of the theaters there was a constant current of antitheatrical sentiment advanced first by the Puritans, sustained by the Baptists and Methodists, and proliferated still later by the Irish Catholics.

In the mid-nineteenth century Methodist and Baptist ministers railed against the moral offense of theater from pulpits literally around the corner from the Boston Museum, where Eichberg's operettas were being performed. In 1876 the Baptists and Methodists, joined by the Episcopalians, formed the Boston Watch and Ward Society, which considered itself the guardian of public morality, banning books and censoring theatrical performances. This group wielded power in Boston up to World War II. The effect of this inimical attitude upon opera performance in Boston was that this major city, with a tradition of strong support for the arts, got a very late start in opera. The 3,000 seat Boston Theater built in 1854 served as the city's opera house until the official Boston Opera House was built in 1909 (it was razed in 1957 and not replaced).

Eichberg's tactics of writing fairly simple music for amateur singers helped him to prevail. *The Doctor of Alcantara* enjoyed relative success: Oliver Ditson announced publication of the songs and overture in May 1862, and Eichberg began touring it in New England in July; eventually the work achieved approximately 500 performances, mainly in the United States, between 1862 and 1918 (Root, pp. 136–40). After the fashion of the most successful European operas, a "Grand fantasie on themes from the opera" was arranged by J.N. Pattison (New York: Wm. A. Pond, 1868). The show had a brief revival in 1988, with performances by The Friends of Dr. Burney at the Museum of Fine Arts, Boston, at Suffolk University, and on the island of Nantucket.

Although John Hill Hewitt's comic opera *Rip Van Winkle* predates Eichberg's first score (see Volume 6 of this series), *The Doctor of Alcantara* was more widely heard and had a greater influence on subsequent musical theater in the United States. During the 1860s the *New York Musical Gazette* (for example, in vol. 1, no. 1, November 1866, p. 5) distinguished between Italian opera, French comic opera, and American opera, with Eichberg's works representing the latter. An article in *Harper's Weekly* (1869) ventured that "Mr. Eichberg . . . may safely claim the title of the first American operatic composer. His operas . . . seem to be as far removed from Offenbach's buffoonery as from the pretentiousness of the modern German school." Eichberg's obituary in *The Boston Journal* (January 19, 1893) affirms his status as a pioneer: "he became known as the first composer of English American operas." In the succeeding century, William T. Upton called Eichberg a man "of outstanding ability and influence" (p. 74). Donald J. Grout offered the opinion that "American operetta and comic opera may be traced from the works of the German-born Julius Eichberg," and the first work on his list is *The Doctor of Alcantara* (p. 493).

The Composer

Julius Eichberg, born in Dusseldorf, Germany (June 13, 1824), attended the Brussels Conservatory where he won first prizes for violin and composition in 1843. After graduation, he was a musical director in German opera houses, then directed an opera troupe in Geneva, was made professor in the conservatory there and Director of Sacred Music at a church. He emigrated to the United States for reasons of his health in 1857. After two years in New York, he moved to Boston in 1859 to become music director of the resident orchestra at the Boston Museum. The orchestra was used nightly, in the British tradition, to provide incidental music between, and for, spoken plays, as well as providing musical accompaniment for operatic repertoire. Eichberg wore several hats as composer, arranger, conductor, and violinist. One of his musicians remembered him as "strict in manner" but a man who "enjoyed jokes," a "strict disciplinarian but rarely overbearing to those under him," "courteous and dignified" (*Boston Transcript*, February 11, 1893).

The Boston Museum, not to be confused with the present Museum of Fine Arts, Boston, was founded in 1841 on the site of the Kimball building on Tremont Street downtown, near Park Street. It doubled as a concert hall and an art gallery, and was one of Boston's premiere centers for musical and theatrical entertainment until its closing in 1903. During the 1860s it was "called the clergy-man's theatre" (Portland, Maine, *Times*, January 22, 1893). The concert hall seated 1,500, but after the first two years it was used mainly for dramatic rather than musical presentations. The galleries displayed paintings as well as stuffed animals, decorative arts, and other "curiosities."

Eichberg composed much original music during his seven years at the Museum, including three operettas: *The Doctor of Alcantara* (1862, with a libretto by Benjamin Edward Woolf), *The Rose of Tyrol* (1863, libretto by F. A. Schwab, after a French operetta), and *A Night in Rome* (1864, to his own libretto, which was published by the Toledo *Evening Blade*, 1871). *The Rose of Tyrol* was something of a departure, written not for the theatrical troupe at the Museum, but for Caroline Richings's English Opera Company, a group of professional touring light-opera performers. The music, hearkening to the Swiss and Tyrolean airs already popular in sheet-music repertoires, was considered superior to the score of *The Doctor*, which the Richings troupe also performed (in San Francisco, New York, Philadelphia, and elsewhere).

During his tenure at the Boston Museum, Eichberg "succeeded in making the modest theatre orchestra a model of its kind" (*Boston Journal*, January 20,

1893). In 1866 he resigned his position, rested a year, and in 1867 he founded and became director of The Boston Conservatory of Music, a still-thriving institution. He based his curriculum upon the European models of Brussels and Geneva (and employed his brother Isadore as business manager). The same year he was elected Supervisor of Music in the Boston Public Schools, a position created for him. (Lowell Mason had been appointed Superintendent of Music in 1838.) Along with Patrick S. Gilmore, Eichberg was "coadjutor" for the 1869 Boston Peace Jubilee, and served as an orchestral leader and composer for the festival. Among his other compositions are published sets of string quartets and books of violin studies. His four-part "national hymn" *To Thee, O Country Great and Free*, written for an 1872 festival at Boston Music Hall with an orchestra of 75 and a chorus of 500 voices from the Boston schools, is today his best-known composition.

He also composed two more operettas, *The Two Cadis* (1868, to his own one-act libretto, with lyrics for several songs by Dexter Smith) and *Sir Marmaduke; or, Too Attentive by Half* (1874, libretto by Woolf). *The Two Cadis* has the most exotic of Eichberg's settings, involving highwaymen in Iraq. It was first performed as a benefit to raise funds for social assistance in Crete. The score, though brief, is Eichberg's most dramatic, praised in the press as having "fluency and grace, . . . ornament, fine finish, and great originality and variety both of thought and treatment . . . , dashing and effective, . . . musicianly in manner . . . . It is no compliment, perhaps, to say that the airs are better and brighter than Offenbach's, for Mr. Eichberg aims higher than mere *opera bouffe*. . ." (unidentified clipping, March 5, 1868, in vocal score, Boston Public Library). The tenor in the first public performance at Chickering Hall (March 5, 1868) was Allen A. Brown, whose collection of music books and scores later became the foundation of the Boston Public Library's exceptional holdings. Of Eichberg's operettas, only *The Doctor of Alcantara* and *The Two Cadis* were published; a manuscript draft and a fair copy piano-vocal score of *Sir Marmaduke* are in the Boston Public Library (**M421.230); the other operettas are lost.

Eichberg was known as "The Music Man" of Boston for a generation. His foremost contribution at the time was as an educator, but a century later we can still enjoy his compositions.

The Librettist

Eichberg's libretto was penned by Benjamin E. Woolf, son of Edward Woolf, a British immigrant musician who led theater orchestras in New York and who wrote several unpublished string trios and violin sonatas. Benjamin Woolf started his career as a journalist, and from 1859 to 1864 was first violinist in the Boston Museum orchestra. Two one-act farces he wrote for Spencer's Boston

Theatre, *Don't Forget Your Opera Glasses* and *Off to the War!*, were published in 1861. *The Doctor of Alcantara* was his first effort at writing for the musical theater; he is said subsequently to have written about sixty plays (one was a five-act dramatization of Dickens's *Bleak House*, entitled *Poor Jo*, in 1876) and translated thirty more. His translations and adaptations of French operettas by Lecocq, Messager, and Audran—some with his own musical additions—were widely circulated, and some of his songs were published. His "musical bagatelle" *Hobbies* (1878) was performed in Boston and New York by Eliza Goodwin's theater company (which was widely identified with *Evangeline*—see Volume 13 in this series), and Wolfe wrote both libretto and music for a satirical comic opera, *Pounce & Co., or, Capital vs. Labor*, performed by Collier's Standard Opera Company at Boston's Bijou Theatre in 1882–83. At his death in 1901 he was music critic of *The Boston Herald*.

The libretto of *The Doctor of Alcantara*, set in the northwestern Spanish village most famous for the Knights of Alcántara, was inspired by a French opéra comique, *Bon Soir, Monsieur Pantalon* (ca. 1851) with a libretto by M. and Mme. Joseph Philippe Simon Lockroy set by Albert Grisar, heavily influenced by the commedia dell'arte as evidenced by characters named Pantalon and Columbine. The dramatis personae of *Bon Soir* are almost identical to those in *The Doctor*. Of the two creators of *The Doctor of Alcantara*, musical-theater historian Gerald Bordman assigns more prominence to Woolf, and relates the show generically to European ballad opera, singspiel, or opera buffa (pp. 20–21). His assessment is reminiscent of an atypical review for an early performance at the Academy of Music in New York, which complained that the music "contains little that is very striking or that insists upon being remembered" but opined that "The plot is excessively amusing and the dialogue sprightly, if not witty" (unidentified, undated clipping, New York Public Library Theatre Collection).

The Work

The Doctor of Alcantara was Eichberg's first attempt at writing a complete score for a musical-theater audience. The press reviews of the first performance were generally favorable. *The Boston Transcript* (April 8, 1862) prophesied "we have had operas called 'American,' and from the pens of resident musicians, before, but this little musical gem inaugurates a new era in at least one class of public entertainment." The Boston music publisher Oliver Ditson brought out the musical numbers of the operetta in piano-vocal score and issued a separate libretto in 1862.

The principal roles are for the doctor and his wife (baritone and soprano) and for their daughter and her intended (soprano and tenor). The daughter's maid (contralto) and a village official (bass) fill out the ensemble numbers, with a chorus of serenaders and citizens. There are minor roles for two porters (baritone and bass) and the tenor's father, whose forte must be comedic stage business for he sings but one line, near the end of the second act.

Eichberg's operetta predated by five years the 1867 American debut of Offenbach's *La Grande Duchesse de Gerolstein*, an event that launched a ten-year vogue of French comic opera. But Eichberg had obviously brought his musical vocabulary with him. *The Doctor* is firmly rooted in western European operatic tradition and contains pointed musical references to European *opere buffe*. The opening serenade in Act I, "Wake! Lady, Wake," is reminiscent of the serenade in Donizetti's *Don Pasquale*, Act III (1843), and the air "The Knight of Alcantara" suggests the "ghost" aria from Weber's *Der Freischütz*, Act III (1821).

The genre designation for *The Doctor of Alcantara* shifted from one moment to the next: "opera," "comic opera," "opera bouffe," "operetta," "light opera," "light operatic entertainment," and beyond. Whatever the label, the essential elements of the work are the spoken dialogue, a romantic plot of light and humorous disposition, and a score written entirely by one composer.

By 1874, when he penned *Sir Marmaduke*, it appeared that Eichberg had composed his last operetta. In an interview with *Dexter Smith's Paper* (November 1874), he asserted that he was "not at work upon any operetta, at present," but that "teaching occupies all my time." Four years later, however, the November 1878 American premiere of Gilbert and Sullivan's "Famous Musical Absurdity" *H. M. S. Pinafore* exploded upon the Boston scene in an unofficial pirated version at The Boston Museum. Its impact was unparalleled. Kate Ryan, a member of the acting company at the Museum from 1872 to 1893, wrote that "the season of 1878 brought about what might be called the transition from the old days to the present" (p. 158). Eichberg regained his inspiration and in 1879 brought out an enlarged, second version of *The Doctor of Alcantara* (which is the version reproduced in this volume). He added two new airs frankly imitative of *Pinafore*: "The Doctor's Song" corresponding to the patter song "When I Was a Lad," to words by George Cooper, who had been lyricist for Henry Tucker's "Sweet Genevieve" and many late songs of Stephen Foster; and a "Scena and Bolero" reminiscent of the Scena in *Pinafore*, "The Hours Creep on Apace." Eichberg's autograph manuscript of the "Scena and Bolero" along with other revisions and additions for the 1879 edition exist in the Library of Congress, tipped in between the pages of his own copy of the 1862 piano-vocal edition, a presentation copy from Ambrose Davenport, Ditson's engraver. The 1879 edition, which is thirty-three pages longer than the earlier version, also includes the stage business and dialogue inserted where it occurs throughout the score. Advertisements for "Ditson & Co.'s editions of New Comic Operas" in some of their 1879 editions pointed out that *The Doctor of Alcantara* "is not a new opera, but is now to take a new start in life, since it is just in the line of the rather easy comic operas that can be brought out either by professionals or amateurs." The 1879 piano-vocal score was reissued by Ditson in 1907.

Not included in this volume is a set of printed orchestral parts (plate number 47277) with musicians' manuscript markings in the Tams-Witmark Collection at the Mills Music Library, University of Wisconsin at Madison, missing the full orchestral score and lacking publisher identification and date. The musical numbers conform to the 1879 version of the vocal score. The parts are for flute, oboe (or clarinet in C), clarinet, two horns, cornet, trombone, timpani, first and second violins, viola, cello, and bass. The Tams-Witmark Collection also contains thirty-five copies of the vocal score, two chorus parts and five promptbooks based on the 1879 score, and six librettos published by Ditson for the 1879 production.

Eichberg's holograph manuscript of the 1862 piano-vocal score, which served as the engraver's fair copy, survives in the Boston Public Library. It lacks an overture, beginning with the tenor serenade "Wake! Lady, Wake." Eichberg made very few changes after this manuscript version had been completed (for this first number, he had not yet added the sharp sign for the D in the left hand in measure 2, nor the staccato marks in the accompaniment when the voice enters, for example), but he did rearrange the order of some of the numbers, and several pasteovers indicate that he reworked some of the ensemble and chorus numbers. Quite revealing is his extensive rewriting of lyrics throughout the show, most heavily in the cavatina "Love's Cruel Dart"; for example, in the first verse of the serenade, he abandons Woolf's line "The lover's enemy the sun" in favor of his own much more evocative "Our enemy the prying sun." Eichberg, it would appear, deserves a measure of credit for the success of the lyrics attributed to Woolf.

In addition to obvious simulations of European comic opera and Gilbert and Sullivan, both versions of *The Doctor of Alcantara* contain favorite nineteenth-century American musical styles: sentimental ballads, parlor songs, a dance-hall tune, and even a bit of melodrama. The seemingly unself-conscious integration of these varied elements is perhaps the most American aspect of Eichberg's work. The score is a reflection of the merging of cultures so characteristic of this country. Although Eichberg had been in America only five years, he must have perceived beauty and value in what he had heard here, and possessed an uncanny ability to assimilate the vernacular style.

It is significant that Eichberg's operettas were performed not at The Boston Theater—the grand-opera house—but at the concert hall-cum-theater of The Boston Museum. These were musical-theater pieces in a popular stage vein, performable by singing actors and accessible to a much broader public in amateur performances. Perhaps for this reason (or because Americans have tended to undervalue its musical products) historians have largely overlooked Eichberg. Julian Mates, enumerating the most powerful influences on the development of American musical theater, cites the post–Civil War Offenbach vogue, Gilbert and Sullivan's 1878 *Pinafore* performance at The Boston Museum, Strauss's *The Lace Handkerchief*, Reginald de Koven, and Victor Herbert. All of these are later than Eichberg's first splash, and the earliest of them are imported goods.

The Doctor of Alcantara joined the repertory of the Richings English Opera Company in the 1860s alongside *La Sonnambula*, *The Bohemian Girl*, *Martha*, and *The Daughter of the Regiment*. Eichberg's obituary in *The Boston Journal* voiced his contemporaries' encomium: "The Dr. of Alcantara, composed in 1862, for the modest musical resources of a theatrical stock company, has not, even in twenty years, lost its wonderful popularity." As the study and documentation of nineteenth-century musical theaters increases, it seems appropriate that Eichberg's pleasing comic operetta be recognized for what it was in its own time: a popular, accessible, musical-theater entertainment, one of the most successful early efforts to develop an American light operatic tradition.

Sources

Plate 1. Julius Eichberg, portrait by G.A. Klucken (undated), courtesy of the American Antiquarian Society.

Plate 2. Poster (n.d.) advertising the various activities of The Boston Museum. Courtesy of the Boston Athenaeum.

Plate 3. Interior of the first Boston Museum, Tremont Street, ca. 1841–46, courtesy of the Boston Athenaeum.

Plate 4. Libretto of *H.M.S. Pinafore*, frontispiece, published for the 1878 production at The Boston Museum, with a picture of The Boston Museum on the cover, courtesy of the Boston Athenaeum.

Plate 5. *The Doctor of Alcantara*, manuscript of "Scena and Bolero," courtesy of the Library of Congress.

The Doctor of Alcantara, score, courtesy of the New England Conservatory of Music.

BIBLIOGRAPHY

Bordman, Gerald. *American Musical Theatre: A Chronicle*. New York: Oxford University Press, 1978; 2nd rev. ed., 1992.

Clapp, William W., Jr. *A Record of the Boston Stage*. Boston: J. Munroe, 1853; reprint, New York: Greenwood Press, 1969.

Eichberg Scrapbooks, Boston Public Library (ML*46.E43S3).

Grout, Donald J. *A Short History of Opera*. London: Oxford University Press, 1947; 3rd ed., New York: Columbia University Press, 1988.

Harper's Weekly: A Journal of Civilization XIII/654 (July 10, 1869): 444.

Mates, Julian. *America's Musical Stage*. Westport, Conn.: Greenwood Press, 1985.

McKay, David. "Opera in Colonial Boston," *American Music* III/2 (Summer 1985): 133–42.

Norton, Elliot. *Broadway Down East: An Informal Account of the Plays, Players and Playhouses of Boston from Puritan Times to the Present*. Boston: Boston Public Library, 1978.

Root, Deane L. *American Popular Stage Music, 1860–1880*. Ann Arbor, Michigan: UMI Research Press, 1981.

Ryan, Kate. *Old Boston Museum Days*. Boston: Little, Brown and Co., 1915.

Upton, William T. *Art-Song in America*. Boston: Oliver Ditson, 1930.

ACKNOWLEDGMENTS

I would like to express my gratitude to the many people who made this volume possible: to Jean Morrow, Head Librarian at the New England Conservatory of Music, and to the librarians and staff of the Music Department of the Boston Public Library; the Boston Athenaeum; the Music Division of the Library of Congress; the New York Public Library; and the American Antiquarian Society. Most especially, I would like to thank the series editor, Deane L. Root, for his contributions to the Introduction and for his inestimable patience and support.

C.R.K.

Julius Eichberg.

Director Boston Conservatory of Music.

Drawn and Printed expressly for "The Folio" by

CHAS. H. CROSBY & CO.

46 Water St. Boston.

Plate 1. Julius Eichberg, portrait by G.A. Klucken.

Plate 2. Poster advertising the various activities of The Boston Museum.

Plate 3. Interior of the first Boston Museum.

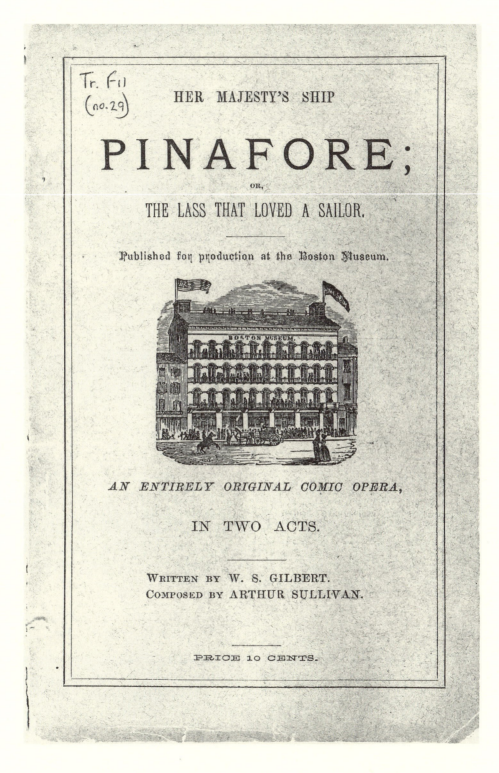

Plate 4. Libretto of *H.M.S. Pinafore,* Boston Museum, 1878, frontispiece.

Plate 5. *The Doctor of Alcantara*, manuscript of "Scena and Bolero," p. 1.

THE DOCTOR OF ALCANTARA

Dramatis Personae

Doctor Paracelsus	Baritone
Senor Balthazar	Baritone
Carlos	Tenor
Perez	Baritone
Sancho	Bass
Don Pomposo	Bass
Donna Lucrezia	Soprano
Isabella	Soprano
Inez	Contralto
Serenaders, Citizens, etc.	

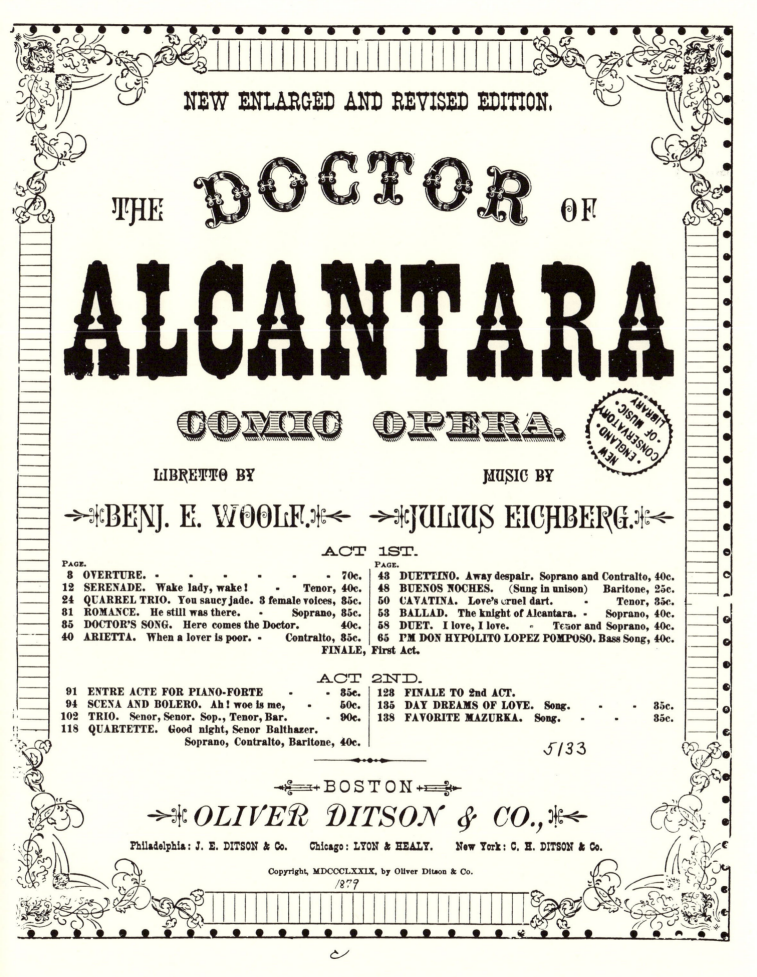

NEW ENLARGED AND REVISED EDITION.

THE DOCTOR OF ALCANTARA

COMIC OPERA.

LIBRETTO BY
BENJ. E. WOOLF.

MUSIC BY
JULIUS EICHBERG.

NEW ENGLAND CONSERVATORY OF MUSIC LIBRARY

5133

BOSTON

OLIVER DITSON & CO.,

Philadelphia: J. E. DITSON & Co.   Chicago: LYON & HEALY.   New York: C. H. DITSON & Co.

DRAMATIS PERSONÆ.

Doctor Paracelsus.
Senor Balthazar.
Carlos . . . . *HIS SON.*
Perez }
Sancho } . . . . *PORTERS.*
Don Pomposo . . . . *ALGUAZIL.*

Serenaders, Citizens, &c.

Donna Lucrezia . . . . . . *WIFE TO DR. PARACELSUS.*
Isabella . . . . *HER DAUGHTER.*
Inez . . . . *HER MAID.*

SCENE: Alcantara in the House of Dr. Paracelsus.

ARGUMENT.

Carlos, the son of Senor Balthazar, has fallen in love with Senoretta Isabella, daughter of Doctor Paracelsus. In the meanwhile, Isabella has been betrothed to a young man, with whose name she has not been made acquainted. Surprised by her mother in listening to a serenade given by Carlos, she confesses her love for him, and refuses to marry the unknown intended. Carlos contrives to have himself conveyed into the house in a basket, under cover of a present to Inez, the confidante of Isabella. Carlos takes advantage of the absence of everybody to get out of the basket and conceal himself. The Doctor and Inez, in trying to hide the basket from the quarrelsome Lucrezia, drop it into the river, and afterwards learn that there was a man in it. Attracted by the despairing screams of Inez, the night watch appear, led by the Alguazil, Pomposo, who informs them that they are under the surveillance of his men as suspicious persons. After the departure of the night watch, the Doctor and Inez are left brooding in fear and dismay over their crime, when Carlos enters, to the great terror of the Doctor and Inez, who immediately suspect him to be a police spy. He discovers himself to them as the son of Senor Balthazar, being at the same time unaware that his lady love and his intended are one and the same. Transported with joy, the Doctor asks him to take a glass of wine with him, which wine, brought by Inez, proving to be one of the Doctor's poisonous decoctions, plunges Carlos at once into a deathlike swoon. The Doctor, believing him dead, and afraid of being detected in this his second imaginary murder, conceals Carlos in a sofa, in which act he is disagreeably surprised by the sudden arrival of Senor Balthazar, who comes to conclude the arrangements for the marriage of his son and Isabella. His presence being objectionable to them, they put every obstacle in his way, so that at length he is forced to pass the night on the sofa, beneath which his son's body is concealed. When he is asleep, the Doctor and Inez, fearful of discovery, enter to remove the body from under Balthazar, who awakes and starts up in fear. Carlos, by this time recovering from the effect of the opiate, contrives to get out of the sofa, and his father meeting him in the dark, utters a cry of alarm which terrifies the Doctor and Inez, and also attracts the neighbors. Mutual explanations take place, and Isabella and Carlos prove to have been loving at cross-purposes, as they were, from the first, intended for each other by their respective parents.

Stereotyped by J. Frank Giles, Boston.

OVERTURE.

JULIUS EICHBERG.

con 8a. ad lib.

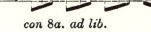

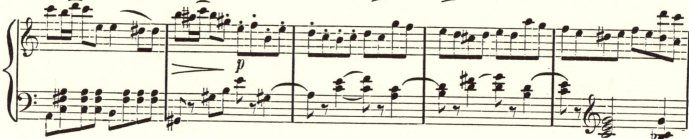

Piu mosso.
8va ad lib.

WAKE! LADY, WAKE.

SERENADE.

SCENE.—*The cabinet of* DOCTOR PARCELSUS.

en - e - my the pry - ing sun, His tire - some course long since hath run, Ah! wake, la - dy
love in - spires my plain - tive strain, 'Tis love a - lone can ease my pain, Ah! wake, la - dy

wake, and rob my heart of care; Wake, la - dy wake, and ease my soul's despair.
wake! I ask one smile from thee! Wake, la - dy wake! and speak of love to me!

The birds of eve now float a - round, And make the air with love resound.

CHORUS.
Tenors.

Wake, la - dy wake, thy lov - er waits thee here, Wake, wake, the hour of love is near.

Bass.

14

* When sung in the Opera go from this sign to the next page, omitting the Symphony.

16

Moderato assai.

Is. The heav'n is spangled with stars; The night spreads her veil o'er the skies; Concealed by the

Luc. The heav'n is spangled with stars; The night spreads her veil o'er the skies; Concealed by the

In.

darkness from all, My lov-er de-sparingly sighs! Hark! Hark! Hark! Hark!

darkness from all, My lov-er de-sparingly sighs! Hark! Hark! Hark! Hark!

diminuendo.

presto.

Luc. (*looking from her door.*)
'Twas Is-abella and I-nez!

LUCREZIA, INEZ, *and* ISABELLA, *enter on tiptoe and approach the window cautiously. As they reach it, they come in contact with each other, and with a cry of alarm rush back to their respective rooms.*

presto.

wake, la - dy wake! I ask one smile from thee! Wake, la - dy, wake! And speak of love to

CAR.

me! The birds of eve now sing around, And make the air with love resound; Wake, la - dy,

CHORUS.

Wake, la - dy, wake! thy lov - er waits thee here! Wake, wake, the hour of love is near.

wake! Wake, la - dy, wake! Wake, la - dy, wake!....... The

Wake, la - dy, wake, the hour, the

hour of love is near,— Wake, la - dy, wake! Thy.... lov - er waits thee

hour of love is near, Wake, la - dy, wake! Wake, la - dy, wake! Thy lov - er waits for thee.

Vivace. Luc. (*looking forth.*)

here. Again that strain? Ah! it must be Some tender swain in love with

Vivace.

pp

me!

Wake,...... la - - dy, wake!........ Wake, la - - dy, wake!

Is. *(looking forth.)*

Again that voice, Oh! can it be The cav - a - lier, the cav - a - lier who followed me!

Car.

In. *(looking forth.)*

Wake, la - - dy, wake! Wake, la - - dy, wake! Again those notes! Ah! it is

Is. Luc. In. Car.

he; Car - li - no sings and waits for me! Hark! Hark! Hark! Wake,

Is, Lu. In. Car.

la - dy, la - - dy, wake! Hark! Hark! Hark! Wake,

la - - dy, la - - dy, wake!

(LUCREZIA, ISABELLA, and INEZ, enter cautiously with dark lanterns, and approach the window. They again come in contact, and as they do so, they open the lanterns, and throw a glare of light on each other.)

dim.

Allegro.

LUC. *(angrily.)*

What means this late in - trusion here?

Is. *(embarrassed.)*

LUC. to INEZ. *(with anger.)*

I on - ly came to take the air!

And you speak out, why this sur - prise?

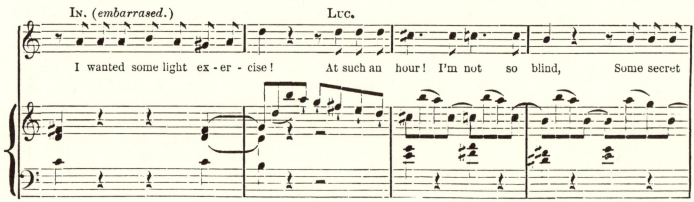

IN. *(embarrased.)*

LUC.

I wanted some light ex - er - cise!

At such an hour! I'm not so blind, Some secret

yet remains be-hind; I tell you that I don't be-lieve you. And do you

And do you

think that we'd de-ceive you!

think that we'd de-ceive you!

Is. (*innocently.*)   Lu. (*embarrassed.*)   Is. (*ironically.*) In. (*saucily.*)

And pray, mama, Why are you here?   I heard your voice.   Indeed!   Oh   dear!

YOU SAUCY JADE!

QUARREL TRIO.

Lucrezia (*to* Inez, *angrily.*)

You saucy jade, Go, get to bed, And let me have no im-pu-dence; Or, sure as fate, If you dare

wait, I'll send you quickly packing hence! You saucy jade! Go, get to

Inez. (*pertly.*)

Why do you, pray, Send me a-way, Have you a rendezvous to-

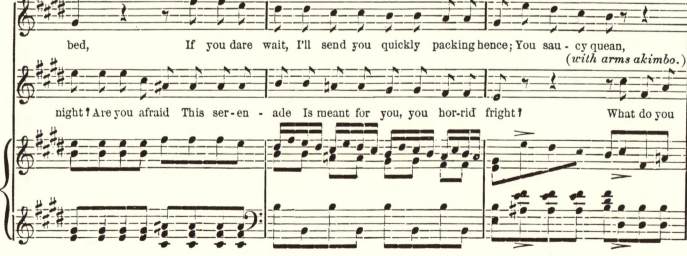

bed, If you dare wait, I'll send you quickly packing hence; You sau-cy quean,

night? Are you afraid This ser-en-ade Is meant for you, you hor-rid fright? What do you

(*with arms akimbo.*)

27

29

Is. (*sobbing.*) What shall I do! Oh, if I knew To whom be-longs this ser-e-nade. A-las! Heigho! One

Luc. hence! You sau-cy jade, Go get to bed, And let me have no im-pudence, Or sure as fate, If

In. soul! Ha, see her storm, she's growing warm. Ha, ha, ha, ha! It's ve-ry droll, Poor tender maid,

Car. (*impatiently.*) Wake, la-dy, wake! Wake, la-dy wake, Wake, la-

Cho. (*outside.*) Wake, la-dy, wake! Wake, la-dy wake, Wake, la-

piu f

thing I know, I am a poor un-hap-py maid, Oh, oh, oh, oh, Un-

you dare wait, I'll send you quick-ly pack-ing hence. I vow, most shameful-ly, I'm used! Was ev-er

This ser-e-nade, Has touch'd her dry and fros-ty soul. Ha, ha, ha, ha! It's ve-ry droll Ha, ha, ha,

-dy, wake, Wake, la-dy, wake!

-dy, wake, Wake, la-dy, wake!

LUCREZIA. Was ever woman so abused in her own house? Holy Saint Iago, protect me from such another onslaught! But you shan't stay another day in my house.

INEZ (*lighting candle on table*). It's too bad if a virtuous girl is to be abused without the privilege of defending herself—all about a paltry serenade too.

ISABELLA. Inez, pray be quiet. Mamma, control yourself.

LUC. It appears that is all I am allowed to control in this house! (*Goes up to window.*)

INEZ. There isn't another maid in all Spain would put up with it; and I'm determined I won't any longer, if I have to live on onions and dry bread for the rest of my existence—carnival days included.

LUC. (*looking out of window*). What do I see? There is a boat almost under our very window. Oh! And that is the cause of all this trouble, is it? Dear me—a serenade must be a very new thing in Spain, to set two silly girls running a race to see which shall be first on the balcony to hear it.

INEZ (*aside*). I wonder if she calls herself a girl too!

ISA. You know, mamma, that you were as eager as either of us to listen to it.

LUC. I listen! Hoighty toighty! It's my belief that Miss Inez has a lover in the city, and that she allows him to come here at this hour, in order to bring our house into discredit,—nay,—to bring me into discredit.

INEZ. No Senora! I know my place better. If I am not Donna Lucrezia, wife of Doctor Paracelsus, I am not a brazen huzzy either. This house, indeed, where there is a young girl engaged to be married.

ISA. (*sighing*). Heigho!

LUC. Why how you sigh at the thought of your wedding!

ISA. Indeed I do!

LUC. Why this is heresy! People have been burned for less. Here you have a husband provided for you without the slightest trouble on your part, and yet you are dissatisfied. While it is the business of every girl's life to allure a husband, you object to one when he is already found to your hand.

INEZ. Perhaps, madam, if I may be allowed to suggest it, she would prefer the usual trouble, and be better satisfied by choosing for herself.

LUC. Be silent, saucebox! I believe you have corrupted her. (*To Isa.*) Why do you object to your intended? He is one of the richest young men in Madrid, and a thorough gentleman.

ISA. A pretty sort of gentlemen he must be to have his wife selected for him!

LUC. That is an especial proof of his trust in you.

ISA. Nonsense! It is an especial proof that he is a fool. Obedience in such a case is no merit.

INEZ. So I say. If he had only been disobedient and refused her, she would by this time have been dying to have him.

LUC. Silence, minion! Isabella, a wealthy lover is not to be despised!

ISA. Heigho!

INEZ. Heigho!

LUC. (*impatiently*). Always sighing! Go to bed. I'll see when the doctor returns, if he can't work some change in you.

ISA. Change! I *won't* change! I *will* be unhappy!

INEZ. Yes, miss, do. Believe me, there is no such happiness for a young girl as misery and despair.

LUC. I see through it all; but let me tell you that you either marry him or go into a convent. What do you mean by objecting to a man whom you have never seen—a man whose name even you don't know? Was there ever such caprice! You have a love for some one else. That is the secret.

ISA. Oh, yes! Such a handsome young man. Of such good family.

LUC. How do you know that?

ISA. Because he is so pretty—so sweet—so amiable!

LUC. A pretty code of morals, indeed! You have had much time to learn him, I dare say.

ISA. It was certainly against my intentions, and while I was at the convent. Oh, so sweet, so pretty!

HE STILL WAS THERE.

ROMANZA.

Beneath the gloom - y Convent wall, Each a - zure night, each ro - sy morn, I saw a

faith - ful shadow fall That filled the air with sighs for - lorn: The night dews

fell o'er him in vain, He feared nor sun - ny sky, nor rain; I seemed to

be........ his on - ly care! Turn where I might, he still was there! He still was there!

His eyes were

like....... the brilliant stars, That night-ly deck...... the sombre sky; His form might

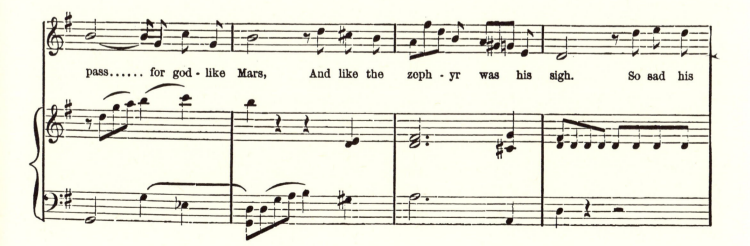

pass...... for god-like Mars, And like the zeph-yr was his sigh. So sad his

mien, it moved my soul;— His fer - vor seemed be - yond con - trol; His voice pur-

-sued...... me every - where: Turn where I might, he still was there! He still was there!

LUCREZIA (*mimicking*). He still was there! Oh, yes! This comes of your reading Gil Blas and Don Quixote, instead of attending to your studies or telling your beads. Holy Saint Martin! what are we coming to? We shall have the Moors again, since daughters are grown so undutiful.

INEZ. If they come in the form of lovers we shan't want the Cid to shiver a lance in our cause.

ISABELLA (*lackadaisically*). Alas! where are those happy times, when after the *Angelus* each day, I found a perfumed billet in the keyhole of the convent gate?

INEZ (*sighing*). Ah!

LUC. What do I hear? (*Indignantly.*)

ISA. A little billet, which breathed the burning and soul-consuming sentiments of passionate and undying love!

INEZ (*sighing*). Ah!

LUC. I'm petrified!—In a convent too! I almost blush!

ISA. What joy to read them! So tender, so respectful, so diffident,

so—so—everything charming! His respect and consideration for me knew no bounds.

LUC. And how did he show it, profligate?

ISA. In his last letter he proposed elopement.

LUC. Very respectful, indeed!

ISA. Yes, and I ought to have accepted it.

INEZ. Now, I call that the height of sincerity.

LUC. What do I hear? I *am* blushing now—I feel it.

ISA. That is love far better than that of a young man I don't know, nobody else knows, and whom I don't want to know, and shan't die if I never do know; and who, moreover, is perhaps very ugly. I vow I *won't* have him if he be ugly.

LUC. What, miss! Do you dare put conditions to your consent?

ISA. Yes; this one, at least.

LUC. It is downright rebellion.

INEZ. No! It's only a declaration of rights!

(*Enter* DOCTOR PARACELSUS, *with morter and pestle in his hand.*)

DOCTOR'S SONG.

Introduced in the

"DOCTOR OF ALCANTARA."

Words by GEORGE COOPER.

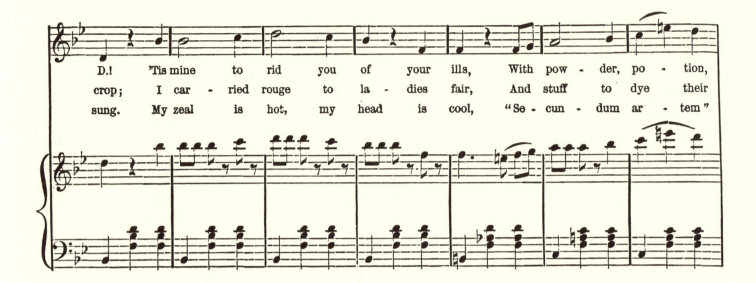

D.! 'Tis mine to rid you of your ills, With pow - der, po - tion,
crop; I car - ried rouge to la - dies fair, And stuff to dye their
sung. My zeal is hot, my head is cool, "Se - cun - dum ar - tem"

plas - ter, pills, My name is fa - mous, too, in sto - ry, And bleed - ing
love - ly hair. To pick up knowl - edge I was wa - ry, And soon was
that's my rule. Com - pound - ing pills, e - lix - ir, bo - lus, I do as -

is my spe - cial glo - ry! In fact, my pa - tients all a - gree, I
dubbed A - poth - e - ca - ry, And that's the rea - son why, you see, I
- sure you I stand "so - lus." To kill or cure, all's one to me, I

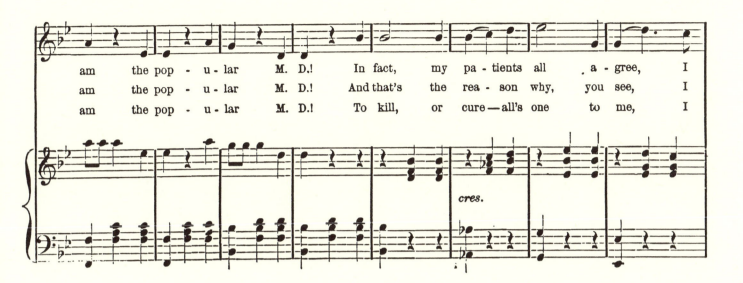

am the pop - u - lar M. D.! In fact, my pa - tients all a - gree, I
am the pop - u - lar M. D.! And that's the rea - son why, you see, I
am the pop - u - lar M. D.! To kill, or cure—all's one to me, I

cres.

At the places marked ⌣, he strikes the mortar he holds in his hand.

am the great, the great M. D.! Stir up the mor - tar, round and round, And

f

with the pes - tle pound, pound, pound, Qui - nine, gamboge — a rousing fee,— I'm the pop - u-

ISABELLA. (ironically.)
He is, he is, he is, he is the great M. D., He is, he
INEZ.
He is, he is, he is the great M. D., He is,
LUCREZIA.
DOCTOR.
-lar M. D. I am, I am, I am the great M. D., I am,
is, he is the great M. D.........
he is, he is, he is the great M. D.! He is, he is the great M. D.
I am, the great M. D.! The great M. D.

(All imitate the DOCTOR.)

Stir up the mor - tar, round and round, And with the pes - tle pound, pound, pound, Qui - nine, gamboge, — a

Stir up the mor - tar, round and round, And with the pes - tle pound, pound, pound, Qui - nine, gamboge, — a

Stir up the mor - tar, round and round, And with the pes - tle pound, pound, pound, Qui - nine, gamboge, — a

rous - ing fee, He's the pop - u - lar M. D.!

rous - ing fee, He's the pop - u - lar M. D.!

rous - ing fee, I'm the pop - u - lar M. D.!

40

Luc. Ah! At last you are returned. Come here, let me tell you what I have just heard.

Isa. My dear sir, I will explain. There has been a serenade here—

Luc. Never mind the serenade. Repeat what you have said to me. You shall hear, Doctor.

Doct. Yes, I hear. (*Becoming deeply absorbed in his bottle.*) Two ounces of white laudanum, and an ounce of distilled lettuce. Yes!

Luc. (*to Isabella.*) Well, my lady! Are you ready? Have you done with this indecision?

Isa. Yes, I *am* decided! I say whatever I am forced to do, my feelings will remain the same. I will be faithful to this hateful intended as—as—long as I can.

Inez. And a very short time at that!

Luc. There! Did you hear that, Doctor?

Doct. (*absently.*) Yes! That was not very bad. As long as she can. He can't expect more than that. (*Becomes absorbed again in his bottle.*) One scruple of inspissated juice of cabbage, and three grains of clarified tallow fat.

Luc. But do you know what all this trouble is about?

Doct. About a young man she is to marry.

Luc. Oh, no! Not at all.

Inez. Nothing like it.

Luc. Silence, minx! It is of a young man she has seen at Seville, and whom she loves.

Doct. Ha! (*Angrily.*) Then she will—(*becomes absorbed.*) Aconite, arsenic, nux vomica, prussic acid! I am afraid I have put a little too much sleep into it for a comfortable sleeping draught. Oh, if I should have made it a poison instead! (*Puts bottle on table.*)

Luc. (*angrily.*) What! Is this all you have to say? A pretty fellow you are to have command of a house. What would become of you if I were dead and gone?

Doct. (*absently.*) I don't know, my dear. You never tried the experiment.

Luc. Bah! Those filthy drugs are all you are fit for.

Doct. We live by them, my dear.

Luc. Yes, and others die by them. I wish I was rid of them!

Doct. (*innocently.*) Wouldn't you like to try my sleeping draught, my dear?

Luc. Bah! You're a brute. (*To Isa.*) As for you, miss, keep your feelings to yourself. Your romance and obstinacy won't do with me in future. I will knock them out of you without any assistance. And you, you minx! (*To Inez.*)

Inez. Ah! now it's my turn.

Luc. I only want examplary people about me; so I give you fair warning. At the first sign of an intrigue on your part, you go!

Inez. Intrigue! Holy Saint Martin, and the echoes in the Alhambra! There is not a more discreet girl in a Spain than I am!

Luc. I don't want discretion.

Doct. No she doesn't. (*Looking angrily at Inez.*)

Luc. I want honesty.

Doct. (*innocently.*) Very much!

Luc. (*going.*) Now, mind! (*To Doctor.*) Ugh! You senseless drug-compounding, villianously stupid, mentally imbecile quack (*Exit Lucrezia, angrily.*)

Doct. (*vacantly.*) Quack!

Inez (*astonished*). Quack!

Isa. (*sobbing.*) Quack!

Omnes. Quack!

Doct. She is not in good temper to-night. (*Goes to cabinet.*)

Inez. Oh, miss! If that should be your lover, who has discovered where you live!

Isa. Do you think he has, Inez?

Inez. Indeed I do.

Doct. (*standing on chair and arranging objects in cabinet*). Inez will you hand me the flacon on yonder table?

Inez. (*paying no attention*). Is he really so fine and gallant a young senor as you say?

Isa. Oh, yes, Inez! Words cannot describe his many perfections Oh, if I am forced into this marriage it will kill me!

Inez. Then don't be forced into it. Kill yourself before hand!

Doct. (*as before.*) Inez, will you hand me that flacon?

Inez. I wouldn't marry a man I didn't love for all the parents in the world. As for taxing me with intrigue, I vow, I wouldn't look in the face of a young man,—especially if there wasn't one near me (*Knock heard at door.*)

Doct. (*still in chair*). I believe there is some one knocking at the door, Inez.

Inez. We all have our troubles, miss.

Isa. I hope you and Carlino agree.

Inez. Oh, yes, miss. We agree very well, but we are not good friends. There is a miff between Carlino and myself, which for bids an approach on either side. (*Knock heard again.*)

Doct. (*aside*). I believe she hasn't opened the door yet. I had better do it myself. (*Exit Doctor.*)

Isa. What! Have you and Carlino quarrelled?

Inez. Yes, miss! He came into money, and from a water-carrier has aspired to be a candy merchant with two mules. The monster is going to eat up his inheritance without me! Oh, miss, the men are all alike!

WHEN A LOVER IS POOR.*

ARIETTE.

* *Instead of this piece, the "Favorite Mazurka," may be sung. See appendix, page 138.*

42

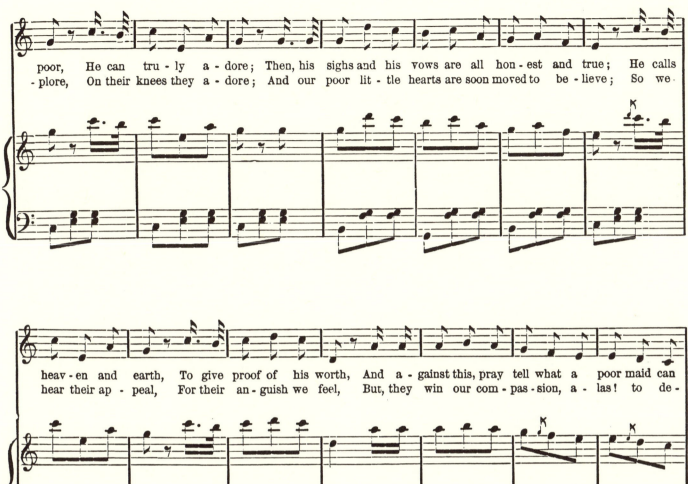

poor, He can tru - ly a - dore; Then, his sighs and his vows are all hon - est and true; He calls
-plore, On their knees they a - dore; And our poor lit - tle hearts are soon moved to be - lieve; So we

heav - en and earth, To give proof of his worth, And a - gainst this, pray tell what a poor maid can
hear their ap - peal, For their an - guish we feel, But, they win our com - pas - sion, a - las! to de -

do! But let for - tune once smile, And his love proves all guile; No more dare you
-ceive.—I have guard - ed my heart Against love's poi - son'd dart, No more to that

trust to a word he can say; For as sure as you're born, You will find his fire gone. Love,
spot can his barb find a way; And I warn you take heed, Of my words at your need. Love,

pp

1o.

burthen'd with mon - ey, Will die in a day! Love, burthen'd with money, Will die in a day!

2o. Allegro.

day.

f

marcato.

cres.

ff

AWAY, DESPAIR!

DUETTINO.

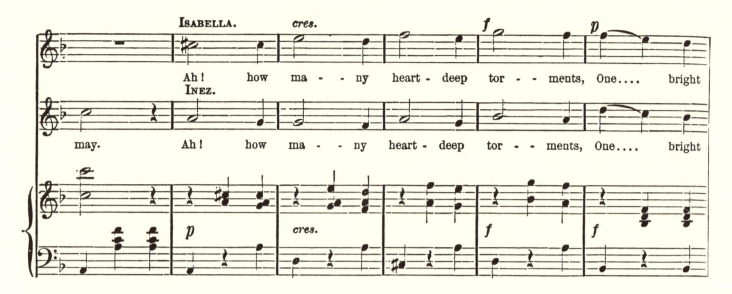

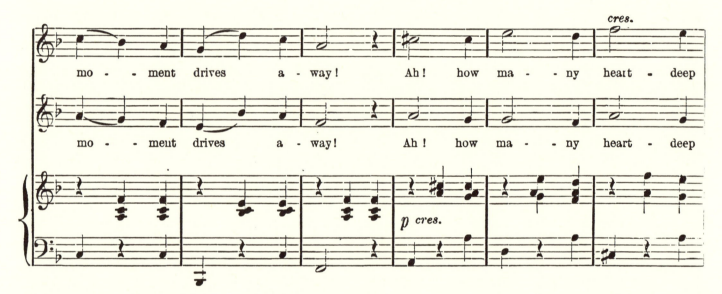

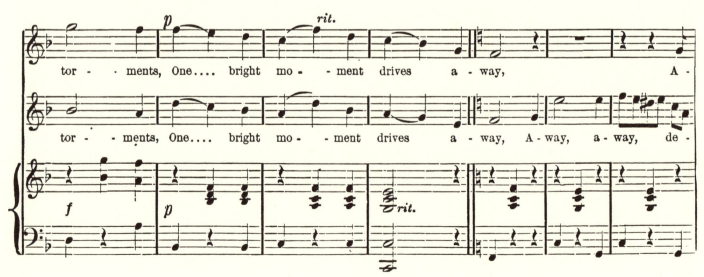

ISABELLA.

A - way, des - pair! for - ev - - er van - ish; Bright - er

INEZ.

dreams shall fill.... my heart: Sor - - row from your bo - - som

ISABELLA.

ban - ish, Bid pale care ... at once.... de - part! Ah,.... how

INEZ.

few.... are hap - - py mo - - ments! Let us seize them while we

INEZ. Alas, yes, miss! Would you believe it, that hateful Carlino has not as much as sent me a paper of candies, the heretic Saracen that he is.

(*Enter* DOCTOR *with* PEREZ *and* SANCHO, *who carry a large basket.*)

DOCTOR. Inez!

INEZ. Doctor!

DOCT. There is something for you, my child.

INEZ. For me?

PEREZ. Yes, for you. (*Winks at* INEZ, *and stands preternaturally solemn.*)

DOCT. Yes, these men have brought it.

PEREZ. Ay!

SANCHO. Yes. (*They grimace at* INEZ *without moving.*)

ISA. Gracious! What do they mean!

PEREZ (*poking his tongue mysteriously in his cheek*). Inez!

SANCHO (*chuckling, and winking his eye*). Inez! Yes.

INEZ. Well?

PEREZ. For you, Inez. This. All right. Hush!

INEZ. What is it?

SANCHO. Nothing. A bijou. The second house on the right hand side.

PEREZ. Yes; overlooking the river.

INEZ. From whom does it come?

PEREZ. From him. For you. (*Winking his eye.*)

SANCHO. Confections. It is a little bouquet of candies.

INEZ. Candies? Oh, it is from Carlino.

ISA. (*sighing*). Heigho! You see he has not forgotten you!

DOCT. Who is this Carlino, Inez?

INEZ. Why—Carlino.—It—comes from Carlino.

DOCT. Oh, yes. I don't know who Carlino is, but I'm glad it's from him. (*To Porters.*) Is there anything more?

PEREZ. This billet. (*Shows letter.*)

DOCT. (*taking letter*). A billet.

INEZ (*seizing letter from* DOCTOR). Yes, for me. Isabella, read it for me. (*Gives it to* ISABELLA.)

DOCT. Yes, my child. Do.

INEZ. Anything else?

PEREZ. No.

INEZ (*taking* DOCTOR's *purse from his pocket and throwing to Porters*). Take this, and go.

DOCT. Haven't you mistaken the pocket, Inez? That is my purse.

INEZ. So it is! Never mind.

BUENOS NOCHES.

PEREZ & SANCHO. (*mysteriously.*)

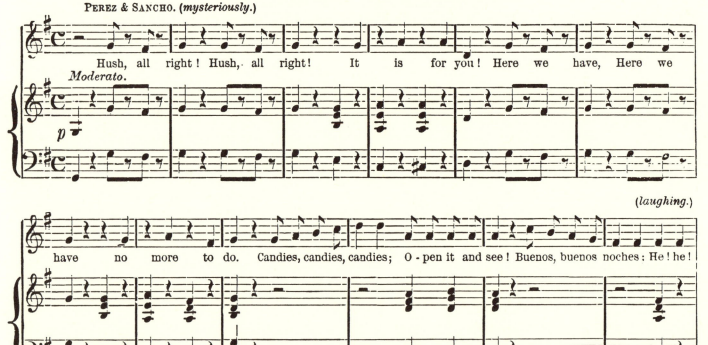

Hush, all right! Hush, all right! It is for you! Here we have, Here we
have no more to do. Candies, candies, candies; O-pen it and see! Buenos, buenos noches: He! he!
(*laughing.*)

he! He! he! he! He! he! he! He! he! he! He! he! he!

(laughing.)

Let us go! Let us go! Our er-rand's done! He! he! he! He! he! he! Don't mind our fun! Candies, candies, candies; O-pen it and see! Buenos, buenos noches; He! he! he! He! he! he! He! he! he! He! he! he! He! he! he!

(they laugh solemnly.)
(Exeunt Perez *and* Sancho.)

Doc. Those are very strange men. There is some mystery here,
Inez. I think so too. Let us open the basket. [Inez.
Isa. (*aside to Inez.*) This billet is for me.
Inez. Indeed! Retire to your room and read it.
Doc. (*trying to open lid of basket.*) What can it be!
Inez. Come with me, Inez, while I read it. I may need your advice. (*going.*)
Doc. Where are you going?

Inez. I heard Donna Lucrezia call us: we will return instantly.
Doc. Do, Inez. I am quite curious to know what Carolino has sent you. (*Exeunt* Inez *and* Isabella.) What the deuce can be in the basket? What a remarkably unfeminine female Inez is! She has no curiosity. Well, I am not so philosophical. (*tries to open basket.*) It won't come open. Never mind. When she returns she will certainly wish to see the contents; so I'll go and get a knife to cut the fastenings. What can it be? I hope it's sausages flavored with garlic. Inez is generous, and I am very fond of them. (*Exit.*) (Carlos *lifts the lid of basket and looks around. He suddenly closes it again.*)

LOVE'S CRUEL DART. *

CAVATINA.

Carlos lifts the lid. (looks around and shuts the lid.)

Carlos gets out of the basket.

CARLOS.

Love's cru-el dart hath to my heart Its passage found; It spurns con-trol, and robes my

soul in grief profound, Oh ! can there be no hope for me Her smiles to gain? Her smiles to

* *Instead of this, the Song " Day Dreams of Love," is often sung. See appendix, page 135.*

-gain? Oh! must she still my bosom fill And cold re-main? The

feath-ered throng whose joyous song Floats thro' the grove, Have each their mate, but 'tis my fate In

vain to love!........ Heigh ho!

Oh! wilt thou not un-to my lot Give some re-lief? Oh! must I sigh un-til I

die Of love lorn grief? Should love like mine, in vain repine, And rend me still? And rend me

still? While anx - - ious care and blank despair My bo - som chill? The

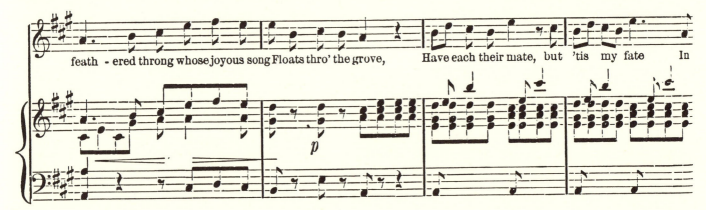

feath - ered throng whose joyous song Floats thro' the grove, Have each their mate, but 'tis my fate In

vain to love!........ Heigh ho!

Car. Ah, some one comes! Perhaps it is she. I will conceal myself again, and wait the auspicious chance. (*Lies down in the basket and closes the lid. Enter* Lucrezia.)
Luc. Inez! Inez! Where has the minx gone? For whom could that serenade have been? Heigho! I fear some giddy swain, careless of his life and honor, has become charmed with me, and thus risks both the one and the other. Well, well; though I condemn, I am bound to pity him. Thank the saints that age has not robbed my heart of its purity or its principles.

THE KNIGHT OF ALCANTARA.

BALLAD.

There was a Knight, as I've been told, Dwelt in a cas - tle strong and old, Its strength all force a - bove;.... He laughed in scorn at

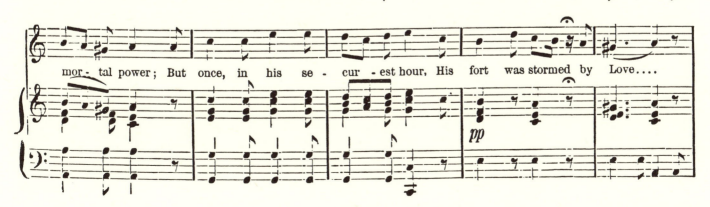

mor - tal power; But once, in his se - cur - est hour, His fort was stormed by Love....

Tra.... la.... la.... la.... His fort was storm'd by Love! Tra.... la....

Piu Lento.

la.... la ... His fort was storm'd by Love! Oh! Knight of Al - can - ta - - ra, No

long - er waves your crest, Your sword and spurs lie rust - - ing, Your lance, too is at

rest. Tra.... la.... la.... la.... Your lance, too, is at rest.......

Tra.... la.... la.... la,.... Your lance, too, is at rest! Gone is the day of

chi - val - ry From out this hap - less, hap - less land, Gone is the day when "La - dye fayre," With

fan and glove in hand, Could win her gal - lant chev - a - lier, To dance the Sar - a -

Tempo di Sarabanda.

band. *(Dances.)* My heart leaps

backward with the strain, And oh! I feel I'm young a-gain. My heart leaps backward

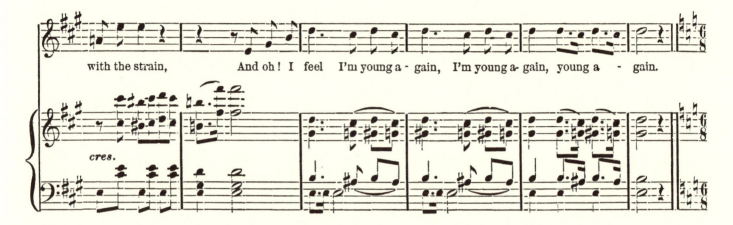

with the strain, And oh! I feel I'm young a-gain, I'm young a-gain, young a - gain.

O gay and gal-lant chev-a-lier, Who nev-er knew what 'twas to fear, Bold

Al-can-ta-ra's Knight. A-las for you chi-

- val - rous youth; Too late you learned the sor - ry truth, 'Tis vain 'gainst Love to fight....

Tra.... la.... la.... la.... 'Tis vain 'gainst Love to fight! Tra.... la....

la.... la.... 'Tis vain 'gainst Love to fight, 'gainst Love to fight, 'gainst

Love to fight.

LUCREZIA. Where can that young man have gone? Perhaps he has drowned himself in despair at my coldness. (*sees basket.*) What is this? (*raises lid.*) A man! What do you want, sir! Don't come near me, or I'll scream. Who are you?

CAR. Señora! Hear me speak. (*coming from basket.*)
LUC. I won't. Go away. Who are you? What do you want? What is your business here?

I LOVE, I LOVE!

DUETTINO.

I love, I love! This is my song by night and day! I love, I love! No pow'r is greater

than love's sway; I love! I love! I love! I love! 'Tis de-li-ri-um ex-treme; 'Tis a phanta-sy su-

-preme; 'Tis an ag-o-ny ca-pricious, And a sky-born joy de-licious! I love! I love! The clouds a-

- bove.... do not the sun more faith-ful-ly o-bey,.... Than I love's sway, than I love's

sway, By night and day, by day and night, Here in my heart he rules by

might. I love, I love! This is my song by day and night. I love, I love! Naught is greater than love's

LUCREZIA.　　　　　　　　　　　　　　CARLOS.

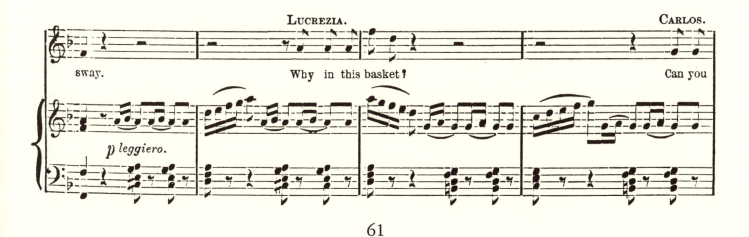

sway.　　　　Why in this basket?　　　　　　　　Can you

p leggiero.

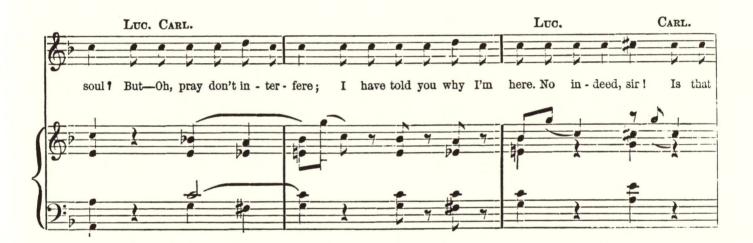

(Very passionately.)

mention! I love, I love! This is my song, by night and day, I love, I love! Naught is greater than love's

LUCREZIA. *(aside.)*

Poor youth! he's doom'd to love in vain, I dare not ease his bos-om's pain. He loves, he

CARLOS. *(With fervor.)*

sway. I love, I love, I love! 'Tis an ag-o-ny de-

loves, he loves! Poor youth, he's doom'd to love in vain, I dare not ease his bosom's

-li-cious; 'Tis a joy and woe ca-pricious. I love, I love, I love!

he loves!   he loves!   he loves! he loves!   he loves!   he

night and day   I love,   I love! Naught is   greater than love's sway.   I   love!   I

loves,   He....................................   loves!

love,   I....................................   love!

Luc. What a fine young cavalier! Sir, do you know that you have done very wrong to enter here?

Car. Yes, Senora. I know it, but I am a tender and sweet young flower of nature, whose heart is a bed of summer roses, wherein the honey yet remains ungathered.

Luc. Oh, Senor, how beautiful and soft!

Car. The summer clouds flit not across the bosom of the sky with greater lightness, than love o'er my heart. Oh, Senora, I adore, I love, I venerate, I worship a person in this house! You will, I am sure, excuse my delicacy, when I forbear to mention her name. You may easily guess who it is, when I tell you she is beautiful.

Luc. (crossing). Oh, he must mean me.

Car. (affectedly). The honeysuckle on its pendulous stem, the little humming-bird sipping sweets from the tender flowers under the golden sky of an Italian autumn, are not more chaste and tender than my love.

Luc. Oh, Senor, I must not listen to this—at least, not just now. You know not the danger you run.

Car. Danger? Who would harm the tender butterfly that spreads his tinted wings to the balmy air of autumn? No, Senora.

Luc. I beseech you, not now. Some other time—some other place. Some one approaches. Oh, sir, retire!

Car. What! Into that basket again? Oh, Senora,—Senorita—Senoritissima! Ask not that. All the saints in the calendar, and the aching bones in my body, cry out against it. Those porters were very kind fellows, but they bumped me unmercifully. I love, Senora, send me not away in despair. Oh, first cut my throat with a pearl-handled penknife, and send my bleeding corpse away, a sacrifice to my overpowering and unhappy love.

Luc. Oh, Senor! Should my husband return—. Consider—get in.

Car. (with one foot in basket). Why do you give me so cruel an alternative? I who love so purely, so warmly, so divinely! (Getting out of the basket.) Senora, have you ever read the story of Prince Camaralzaman in the Arabian Nights?

Luc. If you delay longer I'll scream!

Car. Oh, don't scream! The delicate organization of my cloud-soaring soul will not allow me to survive it. (Gets in basket.)

Luc. (shutting lid on him). Oh, the imprudent young man!

Car. (rising in basket). But——

Luc. (shutting lid on him). Senor!

Car. (rising again). Senora, be divinely kind enough to tell the porters to carry me right side up.

Luc. Yes, Senor.

Car. And pray tell them not to shake the basket too much. The points of the willow are sharp, and puncture me in a very uncomfortable manner.

Luc. (shutting lid violently). Yes, Senor. Oh, what a flutter I am in! I must seek the porters, and get him out of the house as soon as possible (Exit Lucrezia.)

Car. (getting out of basket). What! leave the house without having seen her, without having breathed out my burning soul to her? Never! What shall I do? That is a very nice lady, but I tremble to think that she is neither young nor handsome. How shall I remain in the house? Ah, I have it! (Takes up book.) What is this? Plutarch in quarto (throws it in basket). Seneca in folio (throws in another book). Plato's Philosophy (throws book in). Galen (throws book in). Hippocrates (throws book in). Lopez de Vega, in twenty volumes (throws them in). In they go. (Lifts basket.) It's hardly heavy enough. (Takes up books.) Tragedies! Ah! they're heavy enough. (Throws in a number of books.) That will do. (Closes lid.) Now they may take that away. I'll remain. Where shall I go? (Going.) Where does this lead to? I will explore. (Exit Carlos.) [Enter Inez.]

Inez. The Senora is not here. (Advances cautiously and looks about.) Very good. Now I'll take a peep at my present. Oh, Carlino! What a dear little fellow you are! (Approaches basket.)

Doct. (enters with knife.) Inez!

Inez. Santa Maria! Who is it?

Doct. Only me, my child. What are you about to do?

Inez. Examine my present. I was afraid the Senora would be angry, and so I am going to look at it on the sly.

Doct. Well, I am quite curious to know what you have there.

Inez. Perhaps biscuits. Oh, mercy! Footsteps again.

Doct. It is Lucrezia. It will never do for her to see this, if you wish to keep your place, my child. Take it to your own room.

Inez. (trying to lift basket) I can't. Lend me a hand.

Doct. Where shall we take it? Inez, eat up your biscuits at once, and then we can get the basket away easily enough.

Inez. No! Let us take it out on the balcony, until the Senora is out of the way.

Doct. Good! This is as exciting as an intrigue. (Lifts one end of basket.) Your biscuits are heavy, Inez.

Inez (lifting the other end). Yes. (Drops basket on Doctor's toes.)

Doct. Oh, Inez!—Once more. All right. (They take the basket to the balcony and rest it there.) That will do. Stay! Let me

steady it. (The Doctor, in trying to steady it, lets it fall into the water.) Oh, it's gone, Inez! I'm very sorry!

Inez. Oh, my poor biscuits! How could you be so careless? I declare it has sunk! (Enter Lucrezia.)

Luc. I can't find the porters anywhere. (Sees Doct.) Ah, my husband!

Inez. (sobbing). My poor biscuit!

Luc. My dear, I thought you were out walking.

Doct. No; I shall not go just yet.

Luc. (aside). Where can the basket be? He has gone, then. Since he is safe, I will make a true woman's merit of telling her husband all when he can't revenge himself. (Aloud.) Husband!

Doct. Well, wife.

Luc. Have you seen anything here?

Doct. No. (Aside.) She has seen the basket and misses it!

Luc. Nothing at all?

Doct. Oh! Yes! No! Certainly not! (Confused.)

Luc. A basket, for instance.

Inez (aside). Now for another storm.

Doct. Yes, my dear. I remember a basket. Quite a trifle.

Luc. Did you see what was in it?

Doct. No. (Aside to Inez.) You had better tell her all, Inez.

Inez. It was a little present of candies for me.

Luc. Husband, there was a man in it?

Doct. (staggering back overwhelmed). What!

Inez. (fainting against Doctor). A man!

Luc. Yes, a man, who took this means of entering the house, and of making audacious proposals of love to me; but I scorned his offers, and left the room in search of you, that you might avenge the insult. Is he gone?

Doct. (stupified). I should say he was!

Inez. (aside). Perhaps it was Carlino himself!

Luc. You must be mistaken, wife.

Luc. I tell you, I spoke to him, on this spot, not ten minutes ago, and left him here in the basket. He must have been conveyed out again.

Doct. Yes, decidedly.

Inez. He'll not be conveyed out again in a hurry. (Enter Isabella.)

Isa. Inez! (Aside to Inez.) That note. Ha, ha! I have read it. It was for me, and from him.

Inez. Whom?

Isa. My cavalier. He is here!

Inez. What! In the house?

Isa. Yes. He was conveyed hither in that basket!

Inez. (with horror) What!

Isa. (to Inez). It was he who was on the water.

Inez (aside). He's in the water now.

Luc. Well, do you free me from all suspicion? I don't think he will have the impudence to make another visit.

Doct. I don't think he will!

Inez (shuddering). I hope not.

Luc. Come, Isabella. (Crosses.) How could he have got out?

Isa. But, ma, I don't want to go.

Luc. Come along, miss. I have something to say to you. (Exit Luc. pulling Isabella.)

Doct. (to Inez) Look out of the window. I dare not. Perhaps he is swimming in the basket. It was very large.

Inez (looking out). No. There is nothing. He is gone.

Doct. (nervously). He? Who? Pooh! Do you believe it was a man?

Inez. I know it was. Oh, Doctor, we are murderers!

Doct. What do you mean? You threw him out. It was your present.

Inez. No, Senor Doctor. You threw him out.

Doct. Don't be so positive. I won't inform against you.

Inez. Oh, if we should be found out!

Doct. My blood runs cold at the very suggestion. (The rattling of castanets heard outside.)

Inez. What is that? (Starting with fear.)

Doct. It sounds like the rattling of a dead man's bones.

Inez. Oh, don't talk so Doctor! It's only some street dancers.

Doct. Why do people dance? He can't dance! His dancing days are over!

Inez. I am afraid yours are not. Doctor.

Doct. What do you mean?

Inez. Doctor, I'm afraid your last act in life will be something akin to a dance, without any floor to step on.

Doct. Wretched girl!

Inez (going to balcony and looking out). Ah! (Screams.) Mercy! Murder! I can swear I saw the basket bobbing up and down in the water, as though there were a human being kicking inside to get out, and couldn't. Ah!

Doct. (putting his hand over her mouth.) Be quiet, Inez. You make me feel strangely uncomfortable. Don't scream. You'll alarm the night watch!

Inez. But, Doctor—— I feel I am going to scream again. Ah! (Screams.) Stop my mouth.

Doct. (stopping her mouth). I tell you that you'll alarm the night watch, if you haven't done so already. Hark!

FINALE TO FIRST ACT,

(*The march grows louder, and the tramp is heard outside.* Lucrezia *and* Isabella *look out of window.*)

bye! What shall we say? You fool! Hey dey! They heard you cry. It's all good bye! What shall we

[By this time the tramp has become very loud, and three heavy knocks are heard at door. The DOCTOR and INEZ are paralyzed. A short silence.]

LUC.
They're at the door! They're at 'the door!

IS.
They're at the door! They're at the door!

IN.
say? Hey dey! They're at the door! They're at the door!

DOC.
You fool! They're at the door! They're at the door!

f(Knocking outside.) f(Knocking.) f(Knocking.)

[Three more loud knocks heard. At the sound DOCTOR and INEZ rush across, leaving ISABELLA and LUCREZIA.]

TENORI. (Outside.)
Open! in the name of the king! Open! in the name of the king!

BASSI.

Doc. (*trembling.*) / In. / Luc.

Go, I-nez go!   I thank you, no!   I'm sure there's something

Is.

wrong. I'll find it out ere long! I'll find, I'll find it out ere long! I'm sure there's something

Doc. ⎫
Inez. ⎬ I tremble!
    ⎭

wrong; I'll find it out ere long! I'll find, I'll find, it out ere long. [*Exeunt* Is. *and* Luc.]

[*Enter* Lucrezia, *followed by* Pomposo, *the night watch and neighbors.*]

law! Why did you keep me knocking, knocking at the door? I'm Don Hipo - li-to Lopez Pom-

-po - so, An - to - ni-o, Ricard - o Do - lo - ro - so, A true and faithful servant of the

Doc. (*to* In.)   In.

law, Why did you keep me knocking, knocking at the door? Why did you keep him, Inez? I don't

(*to* Pom.)   Pom.

know! But now you're here, I think you'd bet - ter go. Si - lence all, attend to

me!   But   now, but now, upon your balco - ny,   I heard a loud, a loud and dead - ly

scream!   I heard a   loud, a loud, a loud and   dead - ly scream!   That bal - co - ny, you

Luc.   Is.   Doc. (aside.)

sure - ly dream!   No, he does not, I heard it, too! And I! The deuce! what shall I   do?

Doc. (aloud.)   Luc.

The fact is that there was a cat.   No, no! come, Doctor, none of that!   I heard a

Is. & Luc.

A cry of pain was ve - ry plain, A cry of pain was ve - ry plain!

In.

wasn't! it wasn't, it wasn't, it wasn't, it wasn't, it wasn't, it wasn't, it wasn't, it wasn't!

Doc.

Cho.

A cry of pain was ve - ry plain, A cry of pain was ve - ry plain!

Rom.

Si - lence! Si - lence;

Si - - - - - - lence! I'm Don Hipo - li-to Lopez Pompo - so An-

-to-ni- o Ricardo Do-lo - ro - so, Explain to me the meaning of that cry   I heard but now, but now upon yon balco-

Pom. -ny. No hes - i - ta-tion, al - ter - ca-tion, spec-u - la-tion, dis-pu - ta - tion, Both-er - a - tion, dis-ser-

Luc. & Is. No hes-i - ta-tion, al - ter - ca - tion, spec-u -

Cho. No hes-i - ta-tion, al - ter - ca - tion, spec-u -

-ta-tion, ly-ing or pre-var-i-ca-tion. Hes-i-ta-tion, al - ter - ca-tion, spec-u-la-tion, dis-pu-

-la - tion, dis - pu - ta - tion, hes - i - ta - tion, al - ter-

-la - tion, dis - pu - ta - tion, hes - i - ta - tion, al - ter-

"*Silence.*"

-ta-tion, Bother - a-tion, dis - ser - ta-tion, ly - ing, or pre-va-ri - ca-tion. Ex - plain! Ex - plain!

-ca-tion, spec - u - la - tion, dis - pu - ta-tion. Ex - plain! Ex - plain!

-ca-tion, spec - u - la - tion, dis - pu - ta-tion. Ex - plain! Ex - plain!

INEZ. (*to Pomposo.*)   (*imitates Pomposo*).

To you!   To you!   To you! To you, Hipo- li-to Lopez Pom-po - so, An - to-ni-o Ricardo Do-lo-

-ro - so; I will explain the meaning of that cry   You heard but now, but now upon yon balco - ny!

Know then,   know then,   know then, 'twas I! 'Twas you, but why? 'Twas you, but why?   I

(*mysteriously.*)

wandered there to take the air, And in the moonbeam's waking dream; While thus entranced, my

eye I glanc'd Up - on the wa - ter's quiver-ing gleam; And there be - held a stran - ger felled And

plung'd by ruffians in the stream! I saw no more, But trem - bling o'er, I gave that wild and

piercing scream.

Doc. (to Inez.) The deuce! what is it that you say? Sus-

Oh! horror! Oh! horror! (They run to the window and look out.)

ff marcato. dim. pp

In.(to Doc.)

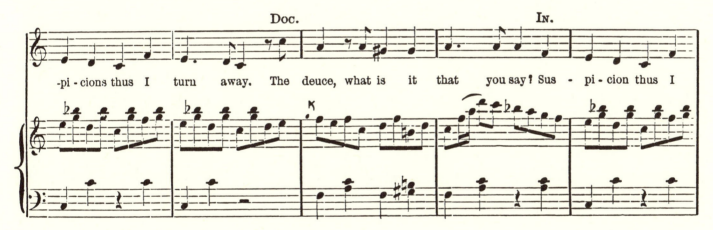

-pi-cions thus I turn away. The deuce, what is it that you say? Sus-pi-cion thus I

Doc. In.

turn a-way! (They come forward again.) Pom. (to Doc.) I thought of something of the sort When

sempre p

8va

Pom.

Threateningly.

I'm Don Hip-o-li-to Lo-pez Pom-po - so, An-to-ni-o Ri-car-do Do-lo-ro - so, I

think, I think I smell a good sized rat, And I will hold you all ac-coun-ta-ble for that.

Luc. & Is. *f*

A - way, A - way, there's some - thing wrong, We'll find it out in - deed ere

In. *f*

A - way, A - way, there's no - thing wrong, You'll find it out in - deed ere

Doc. *f*

A - way, A - way, there's no - thing wrong, You'll find it out in - deed ere

Pom. *f*

Cho. *f*

A - way, A - way, there's some - thing wrong, We'll find it out in - deed ere

f

long, A-way, A-way, there's some-thing wrong, We'll find it out in-deed ere

long, A-way, A-way, there's no-thing wrong, You'll find it out in-deed ere

long, A-way, A-way, there's some-thing wrong, We'll find it out in-deed ere

long, A-way, A-way, there's some-thing wrong, We'll find it out in-deed ere

long, A-way, A-way, there's no-thing wrong, You'll find it out in-deed ere

long, A-way, A-way, there's some-thing wrong, We'll find it out in-deed ere

- way!.......... Come....away, come away, come away, There's something wrong, Come away, come away, There's something wrong.

There's nothing wrong, Come away, come away, There's nothing wrong.

- way!.......... Come.... a-way, come a-way, There's nothing wrong, Come away, There's nothing wrong.

- way!.......... Come....away, come away, come away, There's something wrong, Come away, come away, There's something wrong.

Come a - way, come a - way, come a - way, come a - way,

Come a - way, come a - way, come a - way, come a - way,

Come a - way, come a - way, come a - way, come a - way,

cres.

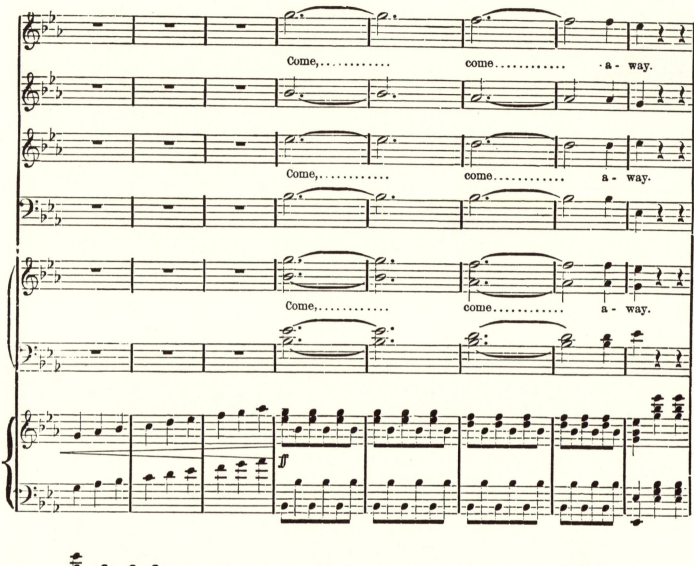

Come,............ come............ ·a - way.

Come,............ come............ a - way.

Come,............ come............ a - way.

(As the curtain falls, POMPOSO prepares to depart. The DOCTOR and INEZ look nervously at each other, and then point to the basket. ISABELLA and LUCREZIA watch them.)

ACT II.

Same Scene as before.   Scena and Bolero. ISABELLA *alone.*

At the rise of curtain, ISABELLA discovered. Scena e Bolero.

AH, WOE IS ME!

(SCENA AND BOLERO.)

Introduced in the
"DOCTOR OF ALCANTARA."

Composed by J. EICHBERG.

Oh! would that fate had cast my lot with him. How hap-py
were my fate, E'en if a small and lone-ly cot our
love from all con-cealed, Each thought of mine to
him be-longs, to him, to him be-longs.

Ah, woe is me. 8.

Oh! would that fate had cast my lot with him, How

hap - - py were my fate, E'en if a small and

low - - ly cot our love from all con-cealed, from all con-

- cealed, from all con-

Ah, woe is me. 8.

- cealed.

Allegro.

ff

dim.

rall.

Tempo di Bolero.

p

But to the

dance, Pleas - ures en - trance, When to the mu - sic all

Ah, woe is me. 2.

sen - ses are yield - - ing, Care dis - ap - pear - ing, Love's vows en -

-dear - ing, And all my soul is full with joy, my soul is full with

joy. To the Bo - le - ro im - pa - tient I'm hast - 'ning,

Mu - sic and joy, Pleas - ure and mirth, all my sen - ses pen - e - trate.

Ah, woe is me.

Mu - sic and joy, Pleas - ure and mirth, All my sen - ses with

bliss pen - e - trate,...... Mu - sic and joy, Pleas - ure and mirth,

All my sen - ses pen - e - trate.   All

2d time turn to the Coda on last page.

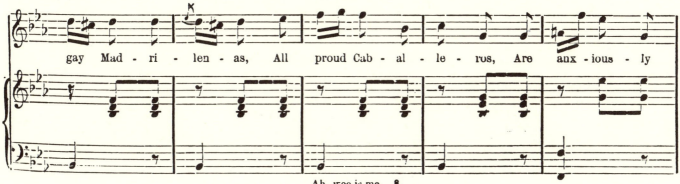

gay Mad - ri - len - as, All proud Cab - al - le - ros, Are anx - ious - ly

Ah, woe is me. 8.

waiting to join in the dance. All gay Mad - ri - len - as, All

proud Cab - al - le - ros, Are anx - ious - ly wait - ing to join in the

dance, to join in the dance, To

join in the dance...................

Ah, woe is me. 8.

Isa. But here comes some one, the Doctor and Inez. I must away! Oh! where can my handsome Cavalier have gone?

Doc. Oh, Inez, why did you throw him out?

Inez. Oh, Doctor, why did *you* throw him out?

Doc. We are all thrown out through it. Poor young man, he must be very wet. (*they go up to window and look out.*)

Enter Carlos.

Car. I cannot stand solitude any longer. It is impossible to conceal myself forever. There is a gentleman yonder. I will speak to him, and declare my love.

Terzetto.—Doctor, Carlos *and* Inez. (*During the ritornello* Carlos *approaches the* Doctor, *and at the end taps him on the shoulder.*)

SENOR! SENOR!

TRIO.

INEZ. Se - nor, still you do not say Why you're here. One mo - ment, pray ! CAR. piu mosso. The eve - ning

air was soft: The sky was calm a - bove; I cast my eyes a - loft, And gave my

thoughts to love; I gazed up - on the moon And id - ly dream'd of bliss; While grateful-

- ly the air Spread o'er my brow its kiss. 'Twas at this time the evening chime Stole on my list'n - ing

me, I wonder who this man can be! His presence sorely troubles me.

trouble seem to be, How strangely do they glance at me! They full of trouble seem to be.

me, I wonder who this man can be! His presence sorely troubles me.

Allegro.

RECIT. INEZ. (*aside to Doctor, with terror.*)

Senor! it it all a plan, I see the ar - ti-

RECIT. CAR. (*with fear.*)

- fice! This honey worded man is an a - gent of po - lice! They eye me

presto.

moment cease your rigor ! Can you harm this pretty figure ? You can-not revenge in - voke, On my pret- ty tinseled

(sobbing.)

cloak ! I am not a thief, be - lieve me ! Real- ly sir, I don't de - ceive you ! A no - ble Se - nor is my

(with an

pa ! A no - ble la - dy is my ma ! Myself am not unknown to fame, And Se-nor Ca-rlos is my name ! Carlos !

infantine voice.) Doc. Car. Inez. Car. Doc. *(surprised.)* Car.

Carlos ! Carlos ! Carlos ! Carlos ! Carlos ! Car - los ! Then you real- ly Car - los are ? The son of Se - nor Bal - tha-

Se - nor Car - los! Se - nor Car - los! Se - nor Car - los! Se - nor Car - los! Se - nor

Be - cause I'm Car - - - - los!

Car - los! Se - nor Car - los! Se - nor Car - los! Se - nor Car - los! His

Be - cause I'm Car - - - - los! This

presence a - larming, sus - picions, dis - arming, We still must con - tin - ue to act out our part. His

conduct is charming, but somewhat a - larming, I can - not di - vine what it means, for my part; This

presence a - larming, sus - picions, dis - arming, We still must con - tin - ue to act out our part. Ah

conduct is charming, but somewhat a - larming, I can - not di - vine what it means, for my part;

Se - nor Car - los! Se - nor Car - los! Se - nor Car - los! Se - nor Car - los! Se - nor

Be - cause I'm Car - - - los!

Car - los! Se - nor Car - los! Se - nor Car - los! Se - nor Car - los! His

Be - cause I'm Car - - - los! This

presence a - larming, sus - picions, dis - arming, We still must con - tin - ue to act out our part. His

conduct is charming, but somewhat a - larming, I can - not di - vine what it means, for my part; This

presence a - larming, sus - pi - cions, dis - arming, We still must con - tin - ue to act out our part, His

con - duct is charming, but somewhat a - larming, I can - not di - vine what it means, for my part, This

presence a - larm - ing, sus - pi - cions, dis - arming, We still must con - tin - ue to act out our part, His

con - duct is charming, but somewhat a - larming, I can - not di - vine what is meant, for my part, This

presence a-larm-ing, sus-pi-cions, dis-arming, We still must con-tin-ue to act out our part, To

con-duct is charming, but somewhat a-larming, I can-not di-vine what is meant, for my part, What

act........ our part, To act........ our part, To

for........ my part, What for........ my part, What

act........ our......... part.

for....... . my........... part.

INEZ. Oh, Senor, we pray that you will remain with us.

DOCT. Yes, and accept our excuses.

CAR. What does this sudden change mean?

INEZ. Why that severe look?

CAR. (*Simpering.*) Excuse me, it was only a smile.

DOCT. (*forcing him into a chair.*) Sit down, sir, I beg.

CAR. (*rising*) But, Senor——

INEZ. Oh, don't rise. We really can't allow you to stand. (*Pushes him into a chair.*) What refreshments will you take? Some cake?

DOCT. (*eagerly.*) What refreshments will you take? Some cake?

INEZ. Wine? DOCT. Ice? INEZ. Bananas? Plums?

DOCT. Peaches? INEZ. Cordial? DOCT. Maraschino?

INEZ. Lachryma Christi? DOCT. Money? INEZ. His bed?

DOCT. My daughter? INEZ. His wife? DOCT. My horses?

INEZ. His carriage? DOCT. My life blood?

CAR. (*terrified.*) What does this all mean? (*Looks with a silly air about the room.*)

DOCT. (*aside to* INEZ.) It *is* Carlos!

INEZ. (*to* DOCT.) I was afraid it was a police spy! Oh, I am so happy.

DOCT. (*to* INEZ.) So am I. But he spoke of the balcony I am not yet certain of him Look how he stares! I will pump him (*Aloud.*) Well, my young friend. You have appeared in quite an unexpected manner.

CAR. Yes, sir, the beautiful stars of eve——

DOCT. Yes I believe you said so before. Ha, ha! (*laughs uneasily.*) I believe you said—ha, ha!—that you were on the water under the balcony——

CAR. Oh, yes. sir! The flowing stream meandered on its peaceful way. The tender flowers had sunk to rest, and——

DOCT. Grace, for the love of the saints! Tell us what you saw.

CAR. (*silly*) Saw?

INEZ. When the Doctor says saw, he means, in fact—saw!

CAR. (*smiling politely*) Ah, now I understand! The vision of brightness stepped on the balcony——

INEZ. That was I

CAR. I have seen nothing else, on my honor. If anything transpired there that I ought not to have seen——

DOCT. But there didn't. (*Aside.*) I still suspect him! (*Aloud*) What refreshment will you take, Senor? Take some wine.

CAR. Oh, sir! (*Simpering.*) Anything. No, sir! Nothing! I—(*Effeminately*) never drink.

INEZ. What! Not water?

CAR. No. That is, sometimes. I live upon the tender dew that Love distils from the rose leaves. Love is my food, love is my drink——

DOCT. Of course. Inez. get him a carafe of love.

CAR. (*aside.*) How strangely he acts! Who can he be? He seemed to know my father's name.

DOCT. You really must take some wine with me.

CAR. Well, if I must—let it be water. Oh, I love water! Water! Sparkling water! Oh, divine liquor! One looks at water—sails on water—swims in water——

INEZ. Yes, and washes in water!

CAR. Yes. Of course—that is—sometimes. (*confused.*)

DOCT. Inez, get me that flagon of wine in the closet. Be careful, and bring the right one. And, Inez, glasses. (INEZ *gets glasses from closet, fills one from flagon, and offers it to* CARLOS *on tray.*)

CAR. Thank you. (*tastes it*) Bah! (*distastefully.*)

DOCT. What is the matter? [this?

CAR. Nothing. (*with politeness and stupidity.*) What do you call

DOCT. Lachryma Christi.

CAR. Yes. It is fine—splendid. Thank you. (*drinks and is disgusted, but tries to smile to* DOCTOR *with politeness.*)

DOCT. Inez, bring me a glassful also.

INEZ. Yes, Senor. (*gives him wine*)

DOCT. (*about to drink.*) Carambo! What is this?

INEZ. Wine, sir.

DOCT. Show me the bottle. (CARLOS *yawns and is in pain.*)

INEZ. There, Senor! (*shows bottle.*)

DOCT. The devil! Have you given him this? It is my medicine. I made it too strong, and it's poison.

CAR. I wonder how you can like such bitter wine. It isn't—very—nice. I feel very sleepy. What—funny—wine! (*falls in armchair.*)

DOCT. Wretched girl, you have done another murder!

INEZ. After all, sir, it is only medicine.

DOCT. Yes, but I intended it for my patients, not for my friends.

CAR. Yes. (*yawns*) My father!—kind man!—funny wine.

DOCT. (*with sublime composure.*) He is dying. We are again accomplices.

CAR. Oh, dear! (*sleeps.*)

INEZ. Gone? DOCT. Dead! INEZ. Very dead?

DOCT. Fortissimo dead. It would have killed an elephant or an alderman.

INEZ. Oh, heavens! Two murders in a night! What is to be done?

DOCT. We must cut the body up, and take it away piecemeal.

INEZ. Let's fling it into the water.

DOCT. No, wretched girl. It would poison all the fish. We have crimes enough on our heads. Inez!

INEZ. Yes! Senor Doctor.

DOCT. You are a murderess!

INEZ. Yes, Doctor. So are you. DOCT. Inez!

INEZ. Yes, Doctor. (DOCTOR *locks doors.*)

DOCT. We are both murderers!

INEZ. Yes, Senor Doctor. DOCT. Inez!

INEZ. Yes, Doctor.

DOCT. We shall be hung if we are discovered. I have always been a kind master to you. Since you have the crimes on your mind, you might as well take the blame of both. Be hung without me, and merit my eternal gratitude!

INEZ. Doctor, I was about to ask you to do the same thing for me.

DOCT. Oh, dear! I feel very cold.

INEZ. How must *he* feel! Oh, St. Peter, have mercy on us! Let us hide the body for the present. Where shall we conceal it?

DOCT. I don't know. The deuce! What do dead bodies mean by trespassing on my house in this way? Here, put it in this sofa-bed. (*opens sofa.*)

INEZ. Yes. Be quick. Help me.

DOCT. I don't like to touch *him*—I mean *it!*—Do you put it in alone.

INEZ. I can't. I won't. Oh, dear! I'm getting faint.

LUC. (*knocks at door.*) Doctor!

DOCT. Oh, mercy! INEZ. We are lost!

LUC. (*outside.*) My dear, some one wants to see you. He has been knocking at the door for some time. (*loud knock.*)

INEZ. It is your wife. Should she see the body!——

DOCT. (*gloomily.*) She must perish too. LUC. (*outside.*) I think it is Senor Balthazar. INEZ. His—I mean its Father.

DOCT. Father! Oh, he must die also. What brings him here?

LUC. (*outside.*) Open the door! DOCT. Yes! Quick, Inez. (*they place* Carlos' *body in the sofa, and close the lid.*)

INEZ. Oh, mercy on us! We are lost. (*opens door, and admits* LUCREZIA, *with candle.*)

DOCT. I'm coming. (*unlocks door, and admits* SENOR BALTHAZAR.)

[ISABELLA *enters.*]

BALTHAZAR (*to* DOCT.) Ah, my old friend! Delighted to see you. Give us your hand. (*shakes* DOCTOR'S *hand.*) Why, how cold your hand is! DOCT. Yes! I've got a cold.

BAL. Ah! I thought I'd take you by surprise.

DOCT. I'm cursed if you haven't. Welcome, my friend! How—how are all your family? BAL. Happily they are all well. (*sits on sofa.*) DOCT. Oh, murder! (*aside.*) He little knows what the padding of that sofa is made of. BAL. My son hasn't been home for some two or three days. But that is nothing.

DOCT. Of course not. I—I—wouldn't feel troubled if he didn't come home for two or three more, if I were you. He is all right.

BAL. Of course. It doesn't trouble me at all. I have just arrived in Alcantara from home. I came down to see you in order to settle about the marriage of which we have spoken so often.

DOCT. Yes—of course. ISA. (*aside.*) I won't wed his son, I'm determined.

BAL. I expect my son here in the morning. I left word to that effect for him, at the hotel, where I knew he has been staying.

DOCT. (*aside.*) Inez! INEZ. (*aside.*) Doctor!

BAL. I suppose I can have a bed here for the night. Eh, old friend? DOCT. Oh, yes. Of course. LUC. Inez, have a bed aired for Senor Balthazar.

INEZ. There is not a bed ready in the house.

LUC. True! I had forgot. Well, he can manage to sleep in this room for the night. We will make it all right to-morrow.

DOCT. (*aside.*) In this room! BAL. Oh, yes! Anywhere will do for me. Don't let me give you any trouble.

LUC. The Senor must be fatigued. Inez, some wine!

DOCT. No. No wine, Inez. BAL. Why not?

DOCT. The—fact—is—I have drunk it all. Ha, ha!

BAL. Ha, ha! Well a little morsel of supper.

LUC. How provoking, to think that of all nights in the year, we should have an empty larder to-night!

BAL. Well, well! Never mind I know it is late. It doesn't matter. I'll take up my bed on this sofa, and wait till the morning.

INEZ. (*with horror.*) Eh? DOCT. (*aside.*) On the top of his own son!

BAL. What the deuce ails them all? They look as if they were going to an auto-da-fe.

LUC. (*aside.*) I wonder where that young man can be?

DOCT. No, no, Senor! Not on that sofa! Really!

BAL. Nonsense! No ceremony! How strangely you all act!

INEZ. (*aside to* DOCT.) Oh, think of his making an unhappy sandwich of his own son!

DOCT. (*aside, tragically.*) It is Providence—Fatality!

LUC. Well, then, Senor, apologizing for our apparent neglect, we bid you good night. In the morning, I hope we shall be able to atone for it.

DOCT. (*to* INEZ.) When he sleeps, we must come here with a pair of shears and cut the body from under him.

INEZ. (*aside.*) Should he wake—— DOCT. (*aside.*) He dies!

ISA. (*aside.*) Oh, why did he come at such an unhappy time? I hate him, as I hate his son whom I have never seen!

BAL. Well, friend, I'll not detain you any longer. Good-night.

GOOD NIGHT, SENOR BALTHAZAR.

In.
(With candle in hand.)

-zar! They will not your slum-bers mar! Good night, Se-nor Bal-tha-zar! Ah!

Se-nor Bal-tha-zar! Ah! Se-nor Bal-tha-zar! May no blood-stain'd corpse af-

fright you, But may an-gel songs de-light you; May no cold and glass-y eye, Moans or

screams of ag-o-ny, Ghosts or fiends, your slum-bers mar! Good night, Se-nor Bal-tha-

(*After Quartetto all exeunt, except* BALTHAZAR.)

BAL. How strangely every body seems to act in this house! What can be the matter! How gloomy every thing is! I don't much fancy this sofa. It's very small! Two would find it rather limited. (*A sigh from sofa heard.*) What is that!—Pshaw!—Nothing. Their miserable good night has given me the horrors, I believe. (*Blows out light, and lies down.*) This house has a very fatal and ghostly air. "Good night!" It sounded very much like "Go to devil!" I must observe them in the morning. (*Takes off his peruke and puts it on wig block on table.*) "May no ghosts your slumbers mar." (*Singing.*) Ghosts, gibbets, bats, murders, moonbeams, moans, screams of agony, and demons! A pretty supper to go to bed on! (*Sings to wig block.*) "Ah! Señor Balthazar!" (*Walking to and fro.*) Can they have any designs on me? They certainly behaved very mysteriously. (*Yawns.*) Pshaw! What a fool I am! I'm very sleepy. (*Sits on sofa.*) I will sleep with one eye open, to be on my guard. (*The wind moans outside.*) Dear me, I feel very gloomy. (*Sings to wig block.*)

FINALE.

calmly does he sleep! My heart with grief is torn. Our crime is dark and deep! We ne'er shall cease to mourn! I

tremble! He sleeps! But should he wake!

Doc.

Have no fear!

(gloomily.)

'Twill be an- oth- er crime, But

fp

Oh! spare him, for my sake! I freeze with fear! A- las! should they overhear!

he must die this time. Come quickly.

Doc. *(speaks.)* "Be cautious." IN. *(speaks.)* "It is not easy, truly." *Vivace.* Doc. *(agitated.)*

(She begins to cut back of sofa with shears.) Take him, take him, take him,

pp

p Vivace.

Lento.

Largo. (CARLOS (little by little gets out of the sofa, and at length sits upon it. The others all group about at the back.

CAR. (dreamily.)

Oh! where am I? I dream! What bliss steals o'er my heart! How came I here? Oh,

dol.

yes! They begg'd I'd not de-part, I'd not depart.—Oh, words de-li - - cious! Oh, hope auspi - -

INEZ.

Yes, try a - gain! Yes, try a - gain!

CARL.

- cious! Oh, words de-li - - cious! Oh, hope auspicious!

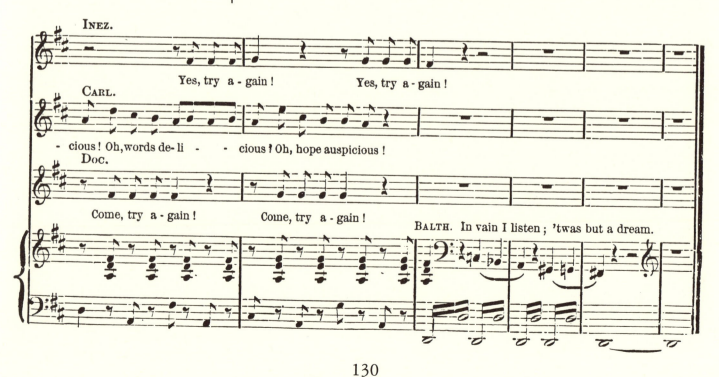

DOC.

Come, try a - gain! Come, try a - gain!

BALTH. In vain I listen; 'twas but a dream.

Luc. & Is. *Allegro molto.*

What does it mean? What does it mean? What does it mean? What does it mean? Speak quickly! Answer now! What

NEIGHBORS.

What does it mean? What does it mean? What does it mean? What does it mean?

means this fear-ful row? Answer! Answer!

Answer!

BALTH. (*seeing* CAR.) What! my son!
CAR. (*to* BALTH.) Ah! my Pa! (*embraces* BALTH.)

Car. **In.** **Doc.** (*to* Inez.)

it was thrown. I'd left.......... it then. What, left it! We may breathe a- gain! You fool! I said

Vivace.

to you, you know, when you were frighten'd, it was not so.

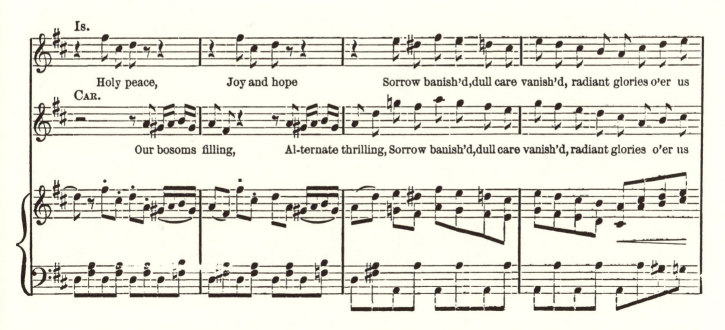

Is.

Holy peace, Joy and hope Sorrow banish'd, dull care vanish'd, radiant glories o'er us

Car.

Our bosoms filling, Al-ternate thrilling, Sorrow banish'd, dull care vanish'd, radiant glories o'er us

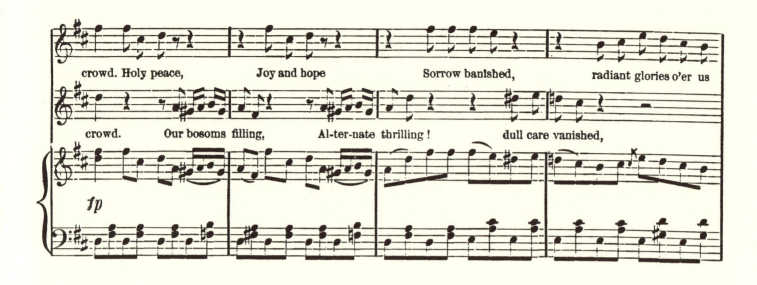

crowd. Holy peace,   Joy and hope   Sorrow banished,   radiant glories o'er us

crowd.   Our bosoms filling,   Al-ter-nate thrilling !   dull care vanished,

fp

crowd.   And our sunshine knows no cloud !   And our sunshine knows no

Hearts beat lightly, Hope smiles brightly ;   Hearts beat lightly, Hope smiles brightly.

Lento. CAR.

cloud !   Hope ev-er smiling When clouds darkest low - er, Sorrow be-

f   *pp Lento.*

Luc. Hope ev-er smil-ing When clouds darkest lower, Sor-row be-guil-ing With sun-shine's gay

Is. Hope ev-er smil-ing When clouds darkest lower, Sor-row be-guil-ing With sun-shine's gay

In. Hope ev-er smil-ing When clouds darkest lower, Sor-row be-guil-ing With sun-shine's gay

Car. Hope ev-er smil-ing When clouds darkest lower, Sor-row be-guil-ing With sun-shine's gay

Doc. Hope ev-er smil-ing When clouds darkest lower, Sor-row be-guil-ing With sun-shine's gay

Chorus. Hope ev-er smil-ing When clouds darkest lower, Sor-row be-guil-ing With sun-shine's gay

Hope ev-er smil-ing When clouds darkest lower, Sor-row be-guil-ing With sun-shine's gay

dow'r Now hovers o'er us, Flying be - fore us, Leading the way un- to Joy's ro - sy bow'r.

dow'r Now hovers o'er us, Flying be - fore us, Leading the way un- to Joy's ro - sy bow'r.

dow'r Now hovers o'er us, Flying be - fore us, Leading the way un- to Joy's ro - sy bow'r.

dow'r Now hovers o'er us, Flying be - fore us, Leading the way un- to Joy's ro - sy bow'r.

dow'r Now hovers o'er us, Flying be - fore us, Leading the way un- to Joy's ro - sy bow'r.

dow'r Now hovers o'er us, Flying be - fore us, Leading the way un- to Joy's ro - sy bow'r.

dow'r Now hovers o'er us, Flying be - fore us, Leading the way un- to Joy's ro - sy bow'r.

DAY DREAMS OF LOVE.

**Introduced in the Comic Opera
The " DOCTOR OF ALCANTARA."**

JULIUS EICHBERG.

Day dreams of love, for - e'er my heart en - tranc - - ing;

Bright wings of hope, a - las. you've sped a - way! Vis - ion of bliss, To

me life's joy en-hanc-ing; Far, far from her, sad long-ing dark-ens my day;

rf *p* *pp*

To me re-turn and heal this fond heart's yearn-ing, Pi-ty for me, for

piu agitato.

hopeless is my fate; Come dear-est maid, For thee my soul is burn-ing,

Must I needs de-spair? Ah! day dreams of love, for-e'er my heart entranc-ing,

rf *f rit.* *f* *p*

Day Dreams of Love—3.

Brightnings of hope, how soon you've sped a - way! Vis - ions of bliss, to

me life' joys en-hanc - ing, A - rise a-new, con - sol - ing an - gels of day!

Vis - ions of bliss, to me life's joys en - hanc - ing,........ A - rise a-new, *cres.*

consol - ing An - gels of day!

Day Dreams of Love—3.

FAVORITE MAZURKA SONG.

Introduced in the Comic Opera
The "DOCTOR OF ALCANTARA."

JULIUS EICHBERG,

ALLEGRETTO.

1. If a lov - er is poor, You may feel quite se - cure; Then his
2. On their knees they im - plore, At our feet they a - dore, And our

sighs and his vows are all hon - est and true. For naught else on
poor lit - tle hearts are soon moved to be - lieve. So we hear their ap -

earth, Can give proof of their worth, Save af - fec - tion sin - cere, and de -
- peal, For their an - guish we feel, But they win our com - pas - sion, a -

-vo - tion to you, But let for - tune once smile, And his love is all
-las! to de - ceive. I have guard - ed my heart Against love's cru - el

dolce.

guile; No more dare you trust to a word he can say, Though the
dart; No more to that spot shall his barb find a way, And I

suit may sur - vive, It will sure - ly not thrive— Love nur - tured in
warn you take heed, Of my words at your need: Love nur - tured in

rich - es will die in a day, If a lov - er is poor, You may

Favorite Mazurka Song. 3.

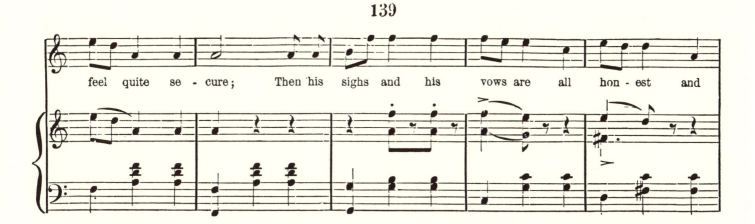

feel quite se - cure; Then his sighs and his vows are all hon - est and

true; For naught else on earth, Can give proof of his worth, Save af-

-fec - tion sin - cere, and de - vo - - tion to you.

Favorite Mazurka Song. 3.

CONTENTS OF THE SERIES

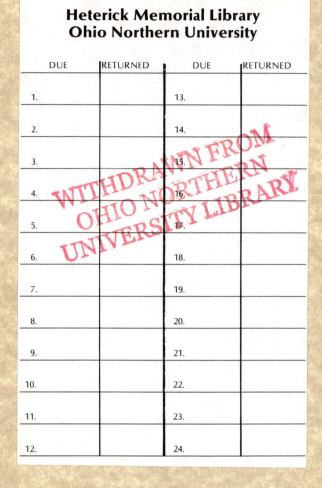